DARK LONDON

Quarto

First published in 2025 by Frances Lincoln,
an imprint of The Quarto Group.
One Triptych Place, London, SE1 9SH,
United Kingdom
T (0)20 7700 9000
www.Quarto.com

EEA Representation, WTS Tax d.o.o., Žanova ulica 3, 4000 Kranj, Slovenia

Text Copyright © 2025 Drew Gray
Design Copyright © 2025 Quarto Publishing Plc

Drew Gray has asserted his moral right to be identified as the Author of this Work in accordance with the Copyright Designs and Patents Act 1988.

All rights reserved. No part of this book may be reproduced or utilised in any form or by any means, electronic or mechanical, including photocopying, recording or by any information storage and retrieval system, without permission in writing from Frances Lincoln.

Every effort has been made to trace the copyright holders of material quoted in this book. If application is made in writing to the publisher, any omissions will be included in future editions.

A catalogue record for this book is available from the British Library.

ISBN 978-1-8360-0424-0
Ebook ISBN 978-1-8360-0425-7

10 9 8 7 6 5 4 3 2 1

Design by Michelle Kliem

Publisher: Philip Cooper
Senior Commissioning Editor: John Parton
Editor: Katerina Menhennet
Senior Designer: Isabel Eeles
Production: Alex Merrett and Chiara Mazzilli

Printed in China

DARK LONDON

A Journey Through the City's Mysterious and Macabre Underworld

Dr Drew Gray

FRANCES LINCOLN

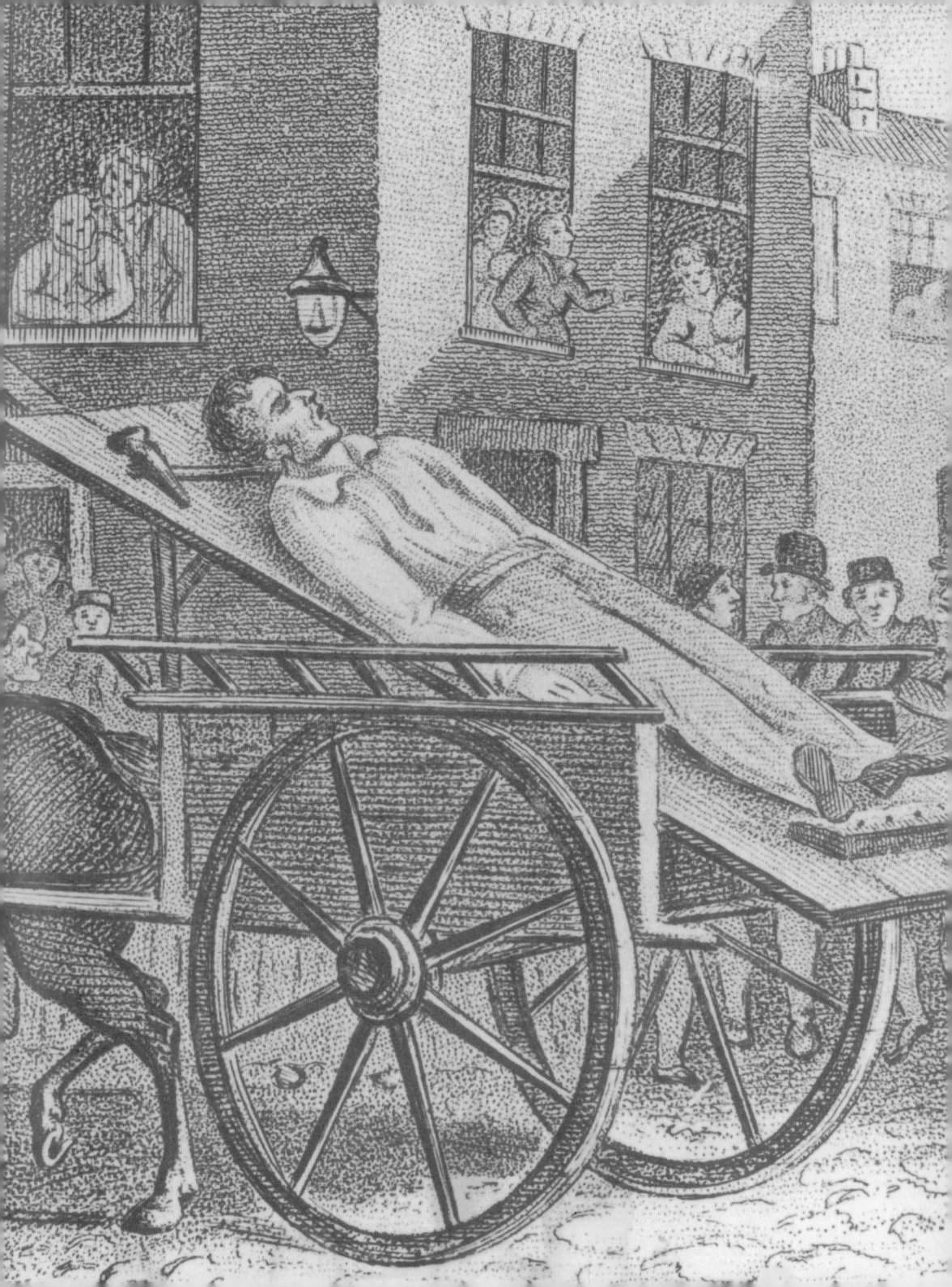

CONTENTS

INTRODUCTION 6

CRIME & PUNISHMENT 12

DEATH & THE SUPERNATURAL 74

DENS OF VICE & INIQUITY 108

DISASTERS & DESTITUTION 142

INDEX 188

INTRODUCTION

This book covers more than 150 years of London's history; from 1750 to the outbreak of the First World War in 1914. During that time seven monarchs sat on the British throne, from George II (who reigned 1727–1760), to George V, crowned in 1910. From Henry Pelham in 1743 to H.H. Asquith (1908–16) there have been thirty-three Prime Ministers. This century and a half saw Britain rise to become the most powerful nation in the world with the largest empire the world had known, and the military muscle required to protect it from jealous rivals. During that time Britain was involved in numerous wars, the most significant of which until 1914 were those against Revolutionary France and Napoleon, the Crimean (against Russia) and the Boer (or South African) War. This then was the era in which the epithet Great Britain mostly clearly represented the reality of her position in the brotherhood of European nations.

Britain's power was built on trade and industry; as the 'first industrial nation' she stole a march on others and benefitted hugely from technological developments like steam power and the railway, but also of course from her long exploitation of enslaved Africans. As Britain industrialised so the great urban centres we know today grew and spread: Birmingham, Manchester, Liverpool, Glasgow and, of course, London, all saw their populations grow and their boundaries expand, swallowing up the surrounding 'green and pleasant land'. Progress came at a price and this would be reflected in the writings of Victorians like John Ruskin and in the Art and Crafts movement led by William Morris. As the so-called Great War approached 'Old England' was fading, to be replaced by the modern in the aftermath of the 'war to end all wars'.

Nowhere was this felt more keenly than in the capital of the empire. Approximately 740,000 people lived in London in 1760 but growth was slow, not helped by a very high infant mortality rate (around 20 deaths per 100 live births in the first 2 years of life). The first reliable census we have registered just over 1 million inhabitants in London in 1801. While fewer infants were dying in the 1800s, growth was driven more by migration to the city from the English regions and other parts of the British Isles and abroad. In 1800, only Beijing was home to more people than London and by 1860, the population of London had trebled to reach 3,188,485, with 38 per cent of those having been born somewhere else. By the time George V ascended the throne the capital's population had reached 7 million. For context, London in 2024 had a population estimated at 9,748,000. So, put simply, in just 150 years the number of souls living in London multiplied tenfold.

This put tremendous strain on the capital and its resources, and brought social problems that had always been present more sharply into focus. London was the first city in England to establish a professional police force, a direct consequence of the rapid spread of urban London. London had more courts, more prisons, more workhouses, more hospitals and more asylums than anywhere else in Britain. Until 1868 when public executions ceased, London was where you were most likely to be able to watch a man (or more rarely a woman) be hanged.

↓ A cloudy view of London Bridge in 1852.

INTRODUCTION 7

London also had more shops, theatres, music halls, pleasure gardens, tea rooms, pubs, gin palaces and brothels than any other town in Britain. It was the heart of empire and trade (the City was the heart of banking then as it remains today) and the centre of culture and entertainment. It was of course, the seat of government and the primary home of the ruling monarch.

London inspired poets like William Blake who wrote: 'I behold London, a human awful wonder of God' and Wordsworth who described the 'endless stream of men and moving things'. Samuel Johnson famously opined that, 'When a man is tired of London, he is tired of life; for there is in London all that life can afford', showcasing the opportunities it offered. By contrast, Percy Shelley wrote 'Hell is a city much like London... [where] There are all sorts of people undone', and many poets and authors reflected the dangers that the capital represented. The modern novelist and historian Peter Ackroyd entitled his account *London: The Biography*, imagining the city

↓ A busy Victorian courtroom.

(as others have) as a living entity, as something greater perhaps than the sum of its parts.

The London docks served the empire and home market, with every kind of produce and commodity one can imagine being loaded and unloaded there. The masts and rigging of countless ships clogged the view across the Thames, London's great artery and the reason why Roman invaders established a city around 47 CE. The Thames was London's main source of water, something that was to become a serious issue in the 1800s, and a dividing line between north and south, helping shape identities which persist to this day. In Victorian London the development of the railway, and in particular from 1863 the underground railway, fuelled expansion into the suburbs, north and south, east and west, and swallowed up villages like Hampstead and Finchley which had been on the periphery of the Stuart and Hanoverian city. London continues to develop rapidly, and as a consequence of this, as well as man-made catastrophes like the Great Fire of 1666 and the Blitz in 1940, and careless, often near philistine town planning since, much of what stood in the eighteenth and nineteenth centuries is destroyed, hidden, or repurposed. It is possible to walk London's streets and imagine the past, but increasingly one's imagination needs to be sharp. Hopefully volumes like this will help remind Londoners and visitors of the rich, if often dark, histories and culture of this most magnificent example of human industry and endeavour.

This book is divided into four themed sections. Chapter 1 focuses on crime, famous criminals and the way society tried to deal with them. Here then are the tales of murderers and career criminals, or daring terrorists and vicious abusers, and of the instruments of punishment used against them. There are anti-heroes like 'Sixteen String Jack', a dandy highwayman who met his end in 1774, or Charles Peace, one of the cleverest criminals of the 1800s. More well-known cases (like the Jack the Ripper murders) are contrasted with less familiar. In Chapter 2 we learn about the supernatural and unusual side of the old city. In its nearly 2000-year history, London has created plenty of ghosts and poltergeists, but also fabricated very many stories based on false sightings and rumours. There is also the very real relationship of a growing city and its 'permanent' citizens, those who have died and must be buried. London has evocative burial grounds and cemeteries which are outlined within these pages.

Alongside the supernatural this chapter looks at some of the key figures contributing to the capital's magical or psychic past.

We then move into the world of vice and the underground in Chapter 3; not the railway network but the often-hidden side of London society in the 1700s and 1800s. This is where we find prostitutes and brothels, gambling clubs and pleasure gardens, resurrectionists and those who chose to challenge society's idea of 'normal'. Finally in Chapter 4 the book looks at perhaps the saddest part of 'Dark London', the misery of the workhouse, the diseases which took so many too young, and the desperation of those who ended their lives violently. Alongside these tales we discover the human tragedies caused by natural or man-made disasters and accidents, whether infamous incidents like the sinking of the *Princess Alice* in 1878 or the bizarre Beer Flood of 1814. Here we also visit Bedlam and Colney Hatch, London's lunatic asylums, and the destitution of the St Giles rookery.

In the gathering of these stories I have searched the records at the London Metropolitan Archives in Farringdon, and the National Archives at Kew. The British Library at St Pancras has a huge collection of material relating to the capital which I've perused at length. No single volume will give a reader everything they need to understand the history of London, but the works of Jerry White, Peter Ackroyd, Stephen Inwood and Steve Roud, among others, are a good place to start. Looking back on the wealth of contemporary material available, the researcher will find Henry Mayhew, James Greenwood, Jack London, Charles Booth and Charles Dickens invaluable. For a lively, accessible and keyword searchable database of London history, I would also recommend the British Library's newspaper archive, and the published proceedings of the Old Bailey, both of which offer fascinating glimpses into London's social, cultural and criminal history, at the click of a mouse.

London is a monstrous place, with history in every building, pavement and garden. Much of that history is dark, unpleasant and challenging. But at the same time it tells us so much about our ancestors, what they believed, how they felt about crime or poverty, or those that were 'other' or different to them. And in learning about the past we can also reflect: hold a mirror up to ourselves and consider how different (or similar) we are to the millions of those who have walked these streets before us.

→ From William Hogarth's series 'The Four Stages of Cruelty' (1750–1). This engraving shows Tom Nero recoiling from the sight of his pregnant mistress, whom he has just murdered.

CRIME & PUNISHMENT

LONDON POLICE COURTS

THE ENGINE ROOMS OF LONDON'S JUSTICE SYSTEM

In 1792, in response to concerns about the availability of magistrates to deal with crime and corruption, the Middlesex Justices Act was passed. Building on the pioneering work of Henry and John Fielding at Bow Street, the legislation created seven 'police offices' across the city. Each was manned by a small team of 'officers' (to mirror Bow Street's 'runners') and overseen by three magistrates retained on a stipend to ensure they were not tempted into corrupt practice.

These offices became police courts, with holding cells, formal courtrooms and policemen seconded from nearby stations. Six days a week, police court magistrates presided over an almost constant flow of defendants brought in mostly by the 'New Police' (established in 1829) to answer charges of drunk and disorderly behaviour, petty theft, domestic violence, fraud, obstruction of the highway, vagrancy, illegal gambling and other minor crimes.

Prosecutions of more serious crimes – burglary, robbery, rape and murder – were also initiated here, with defendants being remanded to a cell for 'more information' to give detectives time to build a case against them. The police courts were also a source of advice and support for working-class men and women who complained about ill-treatment by employers and law officials, and for cab drivers whose fares had refused to pay them. Every day a handful of cases made the newspapers, so all of London (and further afield) could get a taste of life in the courts.

↓ A woman stands in the dock of a London police court.

IKEY SOLOMONS
A LIFELONG DEDICATION TO CRIME

Isaac Solomons was born in approximately 1785, the son of an immigrant from Bavaria. Solomons garnered a reputation as a 'fence' (a receiver of stolen goods) and was twice sentenced to be transported to Van Diemen's Land (Australia). His criminal record is extensive: first appearing at the Old Bailey in June 1810, he was convicted of picking the pocket of Thomas Dodd, taking his wallet and a substantial sum of money. Although he was sentenced to transportation, Solomons went to prison instead.

Released in 1816, he switched from direct theft to receiving, and successfully avoided arrest until 1827. His arrest followed a burglary at Charles Strachan's warehouse in the City, where watch movements valued at £200 (£17,800 today) had been stolen. Solomons' house near Petticoat Lane was searched and five watch movements discovered. However, Solomon's wife and father distracted the officers and Ikey escaped. He avoided capture until April 1827, when he was interred in Newgate Prison with his family to await trial. The police secured evidence of his criminality and the case against him was mounting.

Before he could face the music, he escaped! His wife Ann and his father Henry were not so fortunate; both ended up being sent to Australia. Solomons managed to travel to join them, only to be arrested and sent home. On 8 July 1830 he was convicted of receiving stolen goods and sentenced to fourteen years' transportation. He arrived in Australia at the start of November 1835 and after five years had earned his ticket of leave. He died in 1850 'a poor and lonely man'.

→ Ikey Solomons featured in a contemporary pamphlet.

CRIME & PUNISHMENT   15

← *Pillory, Charing Cross*, Thomas Rowlandson, 1809.

THE PILLORY

WHERE THE GUILTY WERE PELTED WITH ROTTEN FRUIT, OR WORSE…

Abolished formally in 1837 the pillory is one of the more enduring images of public punishment in the capital. From the medieval period onwards, those accused of crimes against public moral or the community were subjected to spells of humiliation and abuse by being locked into a wooden structure similar to the stocks, attached to a pillar, for a set period of time. By the eighteenth century offenders like Daniel Defoe were to stand on temporary pillories like that at Charing Cross which had a revolving platform that enabled the gathered crowd to pelt the unfortunate individuals with rotten fruit and vegetables, excrement, or, worse still, brickbats and stones. The entire experience of those pillorized was determined by what the participating onlookers thought of them and the crime that had brought them to suffer such an unpleasant punishment. Those convicted of certain offences, such as the sexual abuse of children or the procurement of young women and girls for prostitution, could expect little mercy. In 1723 a perjurer who had made false accusation of treason was so badly pelted with mud that he suffocated. In 1756 one member of a gang of thief-takers was stoned to death at Smithfield. Others only just escaped with their lives: a sixty-year-old man convicted of having sexual relations with another man was stripped naked by the crowd before being whipped and covered in mud and dirt. By contrast there were those for whom the pillory could prove a vindication of the actions that brought them to be imprisoned within its grip. Crowds might side with the prisoner in cases of slander or sedition especially if the victim of the person's ire was unpopular, like a local magistrate for example. Famously, in 1703 the pamphleteer and novelist Daniel Defoe was set in a pillory outside the Royal Exchange after he pleaded guilty to seditious libel. Far from being abused the crowd showered him in flower petals while his friends sold copies of his writings! Today the term pilloried means to suffer public abuse and humiliation and is a leftover from this ancient form of punishment.

JOHN 'SIXTEEN STRING JACK' RANN

AN ELEGANT DANDY HIGHWAYMAN

Highwaymen were the celebrity criminals of the eighteenth century, the most famous being Dick Turpin, hanged at York in 1739. Another, John Rann, rose to prominence in 1773 when he and three companions were charged with robbing a Hampstead vintner named Simmonds. The quartet was acquitted after Simmonds failed to identify them in court.

Rann earned a reputation as a womaniser with an extravagant lifestyle, famously wearing silk breeches trimmed with silver-tipped strings. Rann continued his criminality, robbing a man on Hounslow Heath of his watch and his money. Again, Rann was acquitted, playing to the gallery and captivating his audience with his charm, having arrived in court adorned with blue ribbons and carrying a bouquet of flowers.

His luck ran out in October 1774 when he was convicted of robbing the Reverend William Bell in September. His flamboyance (he appeared in the dock in a new suit 'of pea green cloth') didn't save him but it did secure his reputation in an age where highwaymen were sometimes feted as anti-heroes, especially if they 'died game'. Rann fitted that mould and, in part because of competing narratives of his life, he was sometimes mistaken for a 'gentleman thief' a character that captivated the reading public. Sixteen-String Jack was executed at Tyburn on 7 December 1774 supposedly dancing a jig to entertain the crowd before he was 'turned off'. He was just twenty-four years old.

← John Rann in an eighteenth-century alehouse.

THE EXECUTION OF EARL FERRERS
THE MURDEROUS ARISTOCRAT WITH AN UNGOVERNABLE TEMPER

On 5 May 1760, crowds gathered at Tyburn gallows (modern day Marble Arch) to witness one of the most extraordinary and symbolic executions of the period. The vast majority of those hanged were young working-class men sentenced to death for highway robbery, burglary, coining, or a multitude of property crimes proscribed by England's sanguinary 'bloody code'.

But on that May day, a very noble personage was driven to his hanging, dressed extravagantly in silver trimmed silk, by a coach and six horses. Laurence Shirley, 4th Earl Ferrers had been convicted of the murder of his steward John Johnson. Shirley's 'ungovernable temper' made him a poor fit for polite society. His general behaviour, particularly his threatening attitude towards his wife, marked him out and caused the Lords to sanction him. In January 1760, having previously separated from his countess leaving his estate in the hands of agents, he returned for a visit. Convinced that his servants were acting for his wife and against him, he singled out Johnson and shot him. Ferrers made no attempt to escape, admitted his guilt and even demonstrated how he'd executed the shot.

Ferrers was held at the Tower before being tried by the Lords in April. Ferrers' dead body was spared dissection on account of his status and rank, and was buried at St Pancras in an 'unusually deep' grave. Thereafter contemporaries and historians have pointed to Ferrers conviction and death as an example that the criminal justice system of the day made no consideration for class.

↑ Earl Ferrers shoots his steward.

→→ A late nineteenth-century depiction of Earl Ferrers' execution at Tyburn.

CRIME & PUNISHMENT 19

AUSTIN AND GEORGE BIDWELL
A PAIR OF AUDACIOUS YANKEE FRAUDSTERS

In August 1873, a trial opened at the Old Bailey which captured the nation's attention. Austin Bidwell and his older brother George were charged, along with George MacDonnell and Edwin Noyes, with attempting to defraud the Bank of England. Sensationally, the Bidwells were accused of forging a £1,000 'bill of exchange', a huge sum in 1873 equivalent to more than £90,000 today.

Moreover, George had been on the run from the police, before he was tracked down by detectives in Edinburgh. Austin was snared in Cuba by William Pinkerton (he of the eponymous detective agency). All four forgers were American, which added spice to the case in the popular imagination. As the trial unfolded, rumours circulated of a plot to help the accused escape.

The trial lasted just over a week and dozens of witnesses were called. In the end it took the jury just twenty minutes to find them all guilty. Noyes declared he was innocent, MacDonnell vainly tried to defend Noyes but was silenced by the judge. George Bidwell asked for leniency for his brother on account of his age, but again the judge was not interested. He sentenced them to penal servitude for life on account of the 'serious shock' their actions had delivered to public confidence in banking. Both brothers wrote up their memoirs after their release (George in 1887 and Austin in 1892), which have provided us with a fascinating insight into the English prison system.

↓→ Coverage of the trial in *The Illustrated London News*.

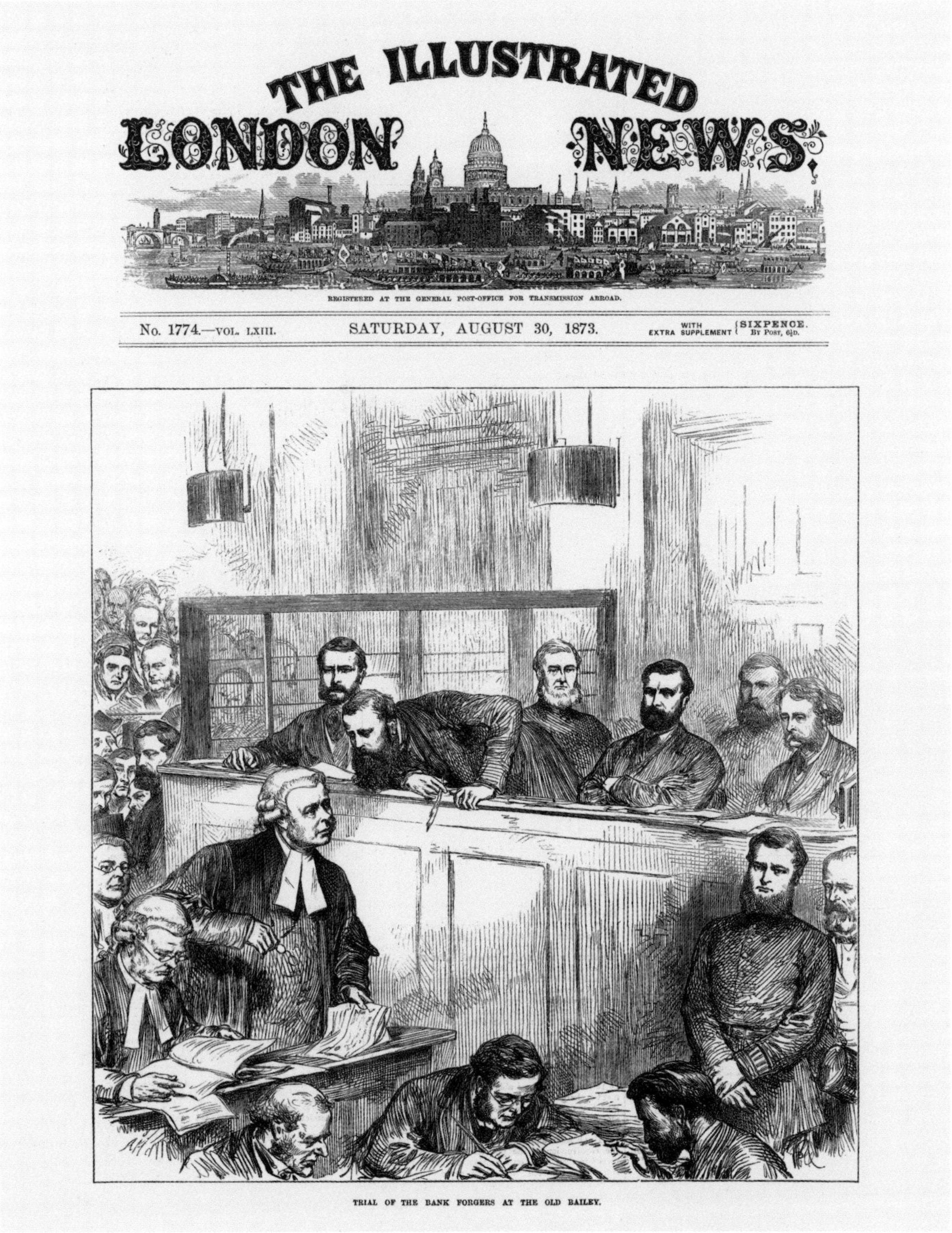

TRIAL OF THE BANK FORGERS AT THE OLD BAILEY.

THE COMING OF THE NEW POLICE
ROBERT PEEL'S 'BOBBIES'

↑ Watchmen attacked by young dandies.

→ A posed photo of an early 'Peeler', note his distinctive top hat and plain great coat.

It is hard to imagine a modern society without a well-organised, hierarchical and uniformed police force, but prior to 1829 one hardly existed. Instead of professionals, semi-amateur watchmen patrolled the capital during the hours of darkness, and part-time parish constables reacted to calls for help from citizens during the day. London (and the rest of the country) was not policed by anything closely resembling a modern police force until the 1830s.

There were entrepreneurial thief-takers, men like the notorious Jonathan Wild or the McDaniel gang (**see page 66**), who operated to catch thieves and reunite missing valuables with their owners for a reward. This was a practice that was open to corruption, which had sprung from the government offering rewards for prosecuting certain sorts of offenders (horse thieves, highwaymen and other serious thieves). Perhaps the best iteration of these men was the Bow Street Runners, created by the Fielding brothers in 1749, who, although no angels, were probably more honest than most.

In 1829 Parliament passed into a law a bill brought by the Home Secretary Robert Peel, apparently with little fuss or resistance. Historians have debated why Peel managed to achieve this when previous attempts to create a central police force had failed. Resistance to formal policing had been entrenched in England since the 1600s, and even after the disastrous Gordon Riots of 1780 (**see page 65**), and the waves of political and social unrest which followed the end of the Napoleonic Wars in 1815, people of all classes instinctively disliked the notion of state-run policing. Put simply, the ideal of English freedom had made

the formation of a uniformed body of police – something commonly associated with France under Napoleon – anathema.

It is possible, likely even, that the growth of London in the 1800s, coupled with the gradual failure of existing semi-voluntary methods of policing, focused minds and allowed Peel, who had previous experience of organised policing in Ireland, to push his scheme into legislation. The result was the Metropolitan Police, or the 'New Police' as they were quickly dubbed: a relatively small force organised hierarchically under the leadership of twin commissioners, one from a legal background (Richard Mayne) the other a former military man (Charles Rowan). As they took to the streets in their blue swallow-tailed jackets and tall stove-pipe hats, swinging their regulation truncheons, and perambulating set beats (like the watch) they drew the attention of a sceptical populace.

They were far from universally popular at first, and had to negotiate their way into everyday life pragmatically. They were a starting point for policing, however, and led to the creation of county forces up and down England and Wales before legislation finally fully established policing in 1856. The presence of 'Peelers' or 'Bobbies' signalled an important shift in the way the British state saw law and order and the government's responsibility for it. It took until 1842 to create a detective branch, and CID was not established until 1878, but policing was here to stay.

↑ Policemen pose outside their station wearing the now familiar helmets which came into service in 1864.

THE DEATH OF POLICE CONSTABLE CULLEY

THE FIRST CRACK IN THE BLUE LINE

In 1833, the Metropolitan Police force was in its infancy. Created in 1829, it had yet to establish itself as a respected institution in the eyes of Londoners. The Met's dual mission was to protect the public and keep the peace, and it was its efforts to do the latter which brought it into conflict with elements of the public on 13 May that year.

In 1832, Parliament passed the Great Reform Act which extended the franchise to many more people. However, while certainly a move in the right direction it did not bring about universal suffrage and so was far from satisfactory to radical groups like the National Union of the Working Classes (NUWC). In protest they organised a demonstration close to Coldbath Fields Prison in Clerkenwell, which was opposed by the Home Secretary (Lord Melbourne) but allowed by the police, who saw no good reason to ban it. However, the police commissioners were keen to avoid a riot and despatched a group of around seventy officers to identify and arrest any ringleaders. By so doing they hoped to decapitate the protest and force the rest of the crowd to disperse with minimal disruption.

Things didn't go as planned; the police, moving forward with truncheons swinging, clashed with protestors and fighting ensued. Sergeant Brooks, a veteran of Waterloo, was stabbed, but not fatally. PC Robert Culley was not so lucky. As he and three officers from 'C' Division crashed into the crowd, Culley was stabbed in the chest. He died later in the arms of a barmaid at the nearby Calthorpe Arms. The coroner's inquest returned a verdict of justifiable homicide, concluding that as the Riot Act had not been read, and no one told to disperse, the police were overstepping their authority.

An Old Bailey jury later acquitted the protestors accused of stabbing Sergeant Brooks, both outcomes a clear statement that the police were not yet accepted by the majority of the populace. PC Culley would go down in history as the first in a long blue line of officers to be killed in the line of duty.

← The Coldbath Fields riot as depicted in Arthur Griffiths' 1899 book *Mysteries of Police and Crime*.

THE LONDON MONSTER

PANIC ON THE STREETS

From 1788 to 1790, a bizarre series of attacks on women precipitated a moral panic as an unknown assailant, dubbed 'the Monster', evaded capture. The attacks were perpetrated by a peculiar individual who confronted women in the street, engaged them in conversation using shockingly indecent language, grinned insanely, before punching and sometimes stabbing them in the thigh or buttocks with a sharp implement.

All of the attacks happened in the evening or at night, with the first victim being Mrs Maria Smyth, a doctor's wife. In January 1790, the Monster attacked two young women, Anne and Sarah Porter, and in June of that same year Anne Porter thought she recognised the attacker in the street. An associate of the sisters set off in pursuit. A search resulted in the arrest of a Welsh artificial flower seller named Rhynwick Williams.

Whether Williams was the 'Monster' or not is moot. The capital was in a frenzy, the newspapers carried every twist and turn of 'monster mania', and a £50 reward had been offered by an insurance broker named Angerstein, so catching someone was more important than catching the actual villain. Williams fitted the profile and he was tried at the Old Bailey in July 1790. Convicted, but with doubts over the validity of the indictment presented against him, Williams was held in Newgate Prison before being retried in December. Again, he was found guilty and sent to prison for six years, where he became a curiosity, visitors paying for the chance to gawp through the bars, or enter his cell to spend some time with the 'monster'.

↑ Williams in the dock at his Old Bailey trial.

THE CAMDEN TOWN MURDER

INSPIRATION FOR A CELEBRATED ARTIST

The discovery of Emily 'Phyllis' Dimmock's body by her lover, Bertram Shaw, ignited one of the most sensational murder mysteries of the early 1900s. Dimmock was a sex worker and she'd been murdered at her home, her throat cut from ear to ear, like Mary Jane Kelly in the Whitechapel series (**see page 30**). To add to the mystery, her bedroom was locked when Shaw arrived, and he had to borrow a key to gain access. The police investigation laboured until handwriting on a postcard in the room, which had been shared by several newspapers, was identified, and an artist named Robert Wood arrested. Wood was tried at the Old Bailey on 10 December 1907, but acquitted by the jury after just fifteen minutes deliberation on the direction of the judge.

The case captured the imagination of the artist Walter Sickert, who painted a series of works inspired by the murder. This has led one writer, the crime fiction author Patricia Cornwell, to suggest that Sickert may himself have been responsible for Dimmock's death, and the murder of five other sex workers in Whitechapel in 1888.

↑ Wood's trial at the Old Bailey. The twelve men of the jury can be seen at the back.

Whitechapel Murders 1888

THE WORLD'S LONGEST RUNNING SERIAL MURDER MYSTERY

In 1888, a series of brutal murders focused the attention of the world's newspapers on London's East End and created the semi-mythical character of 'Jack the Ripper'. The reality is that while several working-class women were murdered, and some mutilated post-mortem, there was never a killer called 'Jack the Ripper'. 'Jack' was an invention of popular culture, born of the fusion of frenzied newspaper coverage and unprecedented public engagement with the crimes.

At least five women were killed, probably by the same person. They were Mary Ann 'Polly' Nichols, 'Dark' Annie Chapman, Elizabeth 'Long Liz' Stride, Catherine 'Kate' Eddowes and Mary Jane Kelly. Their murders took place between 31 August and 9 November 1888. However, research suggests that others on the list of names held in the Metropolitan Police file might also be 'Ripper' victims, including Martha Tabram (7 August 1888) and Frances Coles (13 February 1891). The murders occurred within a tight geographical boundary and in an area – Whitechapel and Spitalfields – which was associated with abject poverty, crime and dense immigrant settlement.

The horror of the murders, which included the mutilation of some of the victims' bodies and the removal of organs, led to immediate assumptions that they were not the work of an Englishman, but a less civilized (as they viewed it) foreigner. Some speculated that the speed at which the killer located and harvested internal organs pointed to him being a doctor or surgeon. Others suggested the murderer must be an outsider to the neighbourhood, perhaps a wealthy aristocratic 'slummer'. These tropes, of the poor immigrant, mad doctor, or decadent milord, have fuelled over one hundred years of discussion as to the identity of the Whitechapel murderer. A long list of suspects has been presented, chewed over, discarded or celebrated, many confirming the popular prejudices and fears of changing eras.

Most likely the killer was a local man, possessed of some butchery skills and very familiar with his environment. He will probably never be conclusively identified, at least not to the satisfaction of the many amateur sleuths who have long debated the case. The murders have left a legacy of popular fascination which has, at times, focused more on the murderer than his victims. But recently, so-called Ripperologists (who investigate the case and its contexts) are more interested in the victims, their lives and world in which they lived, worked and died. Jack the Ripper's transition from reality into folklore is long established, but the desperate lives of those he murdered has been brought more sharply into focus and exists as a reminder that male violence towards women has deep and troubling roots.

WHERE THE CORPSE WAS FOUND IN BERNERS STREET.

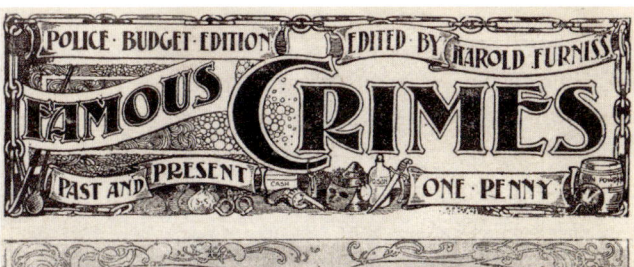

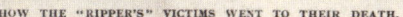

HOW THE "RIPPER'S" VICTIMS WENT TO THEIR DEATH.

← ↑ →→ Jack the Ripper and the search for him quickly became a feature of Victorian popular culture.

←← A contemporary sketch of Dutfield's Yard, where Elizabeth Stride was murdered.

JAMES GREENACRE
ONE OF THE BLACK MUSEUM'S MORE UNSAVOURY CHARACTERS

At the Metropolitan Police's Black Museum (which is, sadly, off limits to the public) there is a macabre collection of plaster of Paris death masks of executed felons. One of the earliest of these is that of James Greenacre, hanged outside Newgate Prison on 2 May 1837, a month before Queen Victoria ascended the throne.

Greenacre had started a relationship with Hannah Brown but, despite proposing marriage and a life overseas, he was only ever interested in acquiring her fortune. When he and his fiancé failed to turn up for their own wedding on Christmas Day 1836, their friends were puzzled and not a little concerned, and challenged him. Greenacre brazenly explained that having discovered Hannah's fortune to be a myth, and that she'd lied to him, he'd broken the engagement off. The truth was that Greenacre had murdered Hannah Brown and then dismembered and disposed of her body, possibly with the help of his mistress Sarah Gale.

On 28 December a labourer discovered a headless female torso, wrapped in sacking, on Edgware Road. Soon afterwards a head turned up in the Regent's Canal, and at the end of January the body was completed when legs were found at Camberwell. The preserved head was displayed in the hope the woman could be identified, which Hannah Brown's brother eventually did. Greenacre and Gale were arrested, put on trial and convicted. As an accessory, Gale escaped the noose but was transported to Australia for life, while Greenacre was hanged and his death mask taken for posterity.

↓ James Greenacre and his lover, Sarah Gale.

THE CLERKENWELL BOMBING AND THE DYNAMITARDS

FENIAN OUTRAGE IN THE VICTORIAN CAPITAL

On 13 December 1867, twelve Londoners were killed and dozens more injured when a crude bomb went off outside Clerkenwell Prison. The bombers' intention was to blast a hole in the prison wall to allow Irish republicans (then termed 'Fenians') to escape. The bombers failed because no one escaped, but in the aftermath eight Irishmen were rounded up and charged with what *The Times* newspaper declared was an act of 'unexampled atrocity'. Only one man, Michael Barrett, paid the ultimate price for the bombing. He was hanged outside Newgate Prison on 26 May 1868, the last person to be publicly executed in England.

If the British state thought this would put an end to the cause of Irish Republicanism they were to be disappointed. While there was a lull of around fifteen years, a terror campaign was reignited in the 1880s, and London was again targeted. From March 1881 there was a series of attempted bombings, some of which failed or were foiled. In May 1884 two devices were exploded: one at the Junior Carlton Club in St James, the other at Scotland Yard, right under the noses of the Special (Irish) Branch, the unit specifically formed to counter Fenian terrorism. Also in May, a bomb was left in a suitcase in

→ A newspaper sketch of the scene of the explosion at Clerkenwell Prison.

Trafalgar Square, where two small boys were kicking it around like a football! Thankfully, an alert policeman retrieved it before it could explode. An attempt to blow up London Bridge in December 1884 ended in only the bombers' deaths. Terror struck again on 2 January 1885 on the underground railway. As a Metropolitan Line train from Aldgate approached Gower Street station a 'large explosion ripped through the carriages, knocking out windows and putting out the gas lights', newspapers reported. Fortunately, no one was badly hurt.

On 24 January, bombs were placed at the Tower of London and in Parliament. A policeman was injured when the latter device exploded as he was bravely carrying it to safety. In the White Tower, where the Armoury displays attracted crowds of visitors, a bomb went off at 2 p.m. but did little damage. Two men, Harry Burton and James Gilbert Cunningham, were convicted at the Old Bailey after an investigation led by Detective Inspector Frederick Abberline, who would later play a leading role in chasing Jack the Ripper. Both men escaped the noose, but went to prison for life. The spate of Irish terrorism had earlier prompted the government to create the Special Irish Branch of police, which later dropped 'Irish' and became simply, Special Branch.

HENRY WAINWRIGHT

ONE OF THE GREATEST
SCOUNDRELS THAT EVER EXISTED

Alfred Stokes was happy to help his old employer move premises in September 1875. But as he stood waiting for a cab outside 215 Whitechapel Road, he felt uneasy. Henry Wainwright, an outwardly respectable East End brush maker, had asked Stokes to carry two large sacks he said contained old brushes. They smelled really bad, and when Stokes peeked inside, he was horrified to find a decaying human head staring up at him! A further search unearthed an arm.

As Wainwright arrived in a cab, Stokes was in a state of indecision. In fear, Stokes bundled the parcels into the cab but followed on foot. He tried to alert two policemen, shouting: 'That cab – stop it – murder – two parcels', but was ignored. When the vehicle arrived in Borough, Stokes persuaded police to investigate. An officer stopped Wainwright, who tried to bribe him. A search of the parcels confirmed Stokes's grim discovery.

At Wainwright's Whitechapel shop, evidence implicated Wainwright in the murder of an unknown woman. But who was she? A man called William Taylor came forward to say that his sister-in-law Harriett Lane had been in a relationship with Wainwright before she had mysteriously disappeared a year earlier. He identified Harriett from her wedding ring and earrings. Wainwright had shot her then cut her up and buried her under the floorboards. His trial lasted a week before he was convicted and sentenced to hang, and his brother Thomas found guilty as an accessory. Lord Chief Justice Cockburn described him as 'one the greatest scoundrels that ever existed'.

→ 'The Whitechapel Tragedy' was how the murder was represented in the press at the time.

THE PENNY ILLUSTRATED PAPER AND ILLUSTRATED TIMES

No. 734. LONDON, SEPTEMBER 25, 1875. VOL. XXIX.

THE WHITECHAPEL TRAGEDY: SKETCHES BY OUR SPECIAL ARTIST.
(SEE "THE POLICE ON THE TRAIL," PAGE 196.)

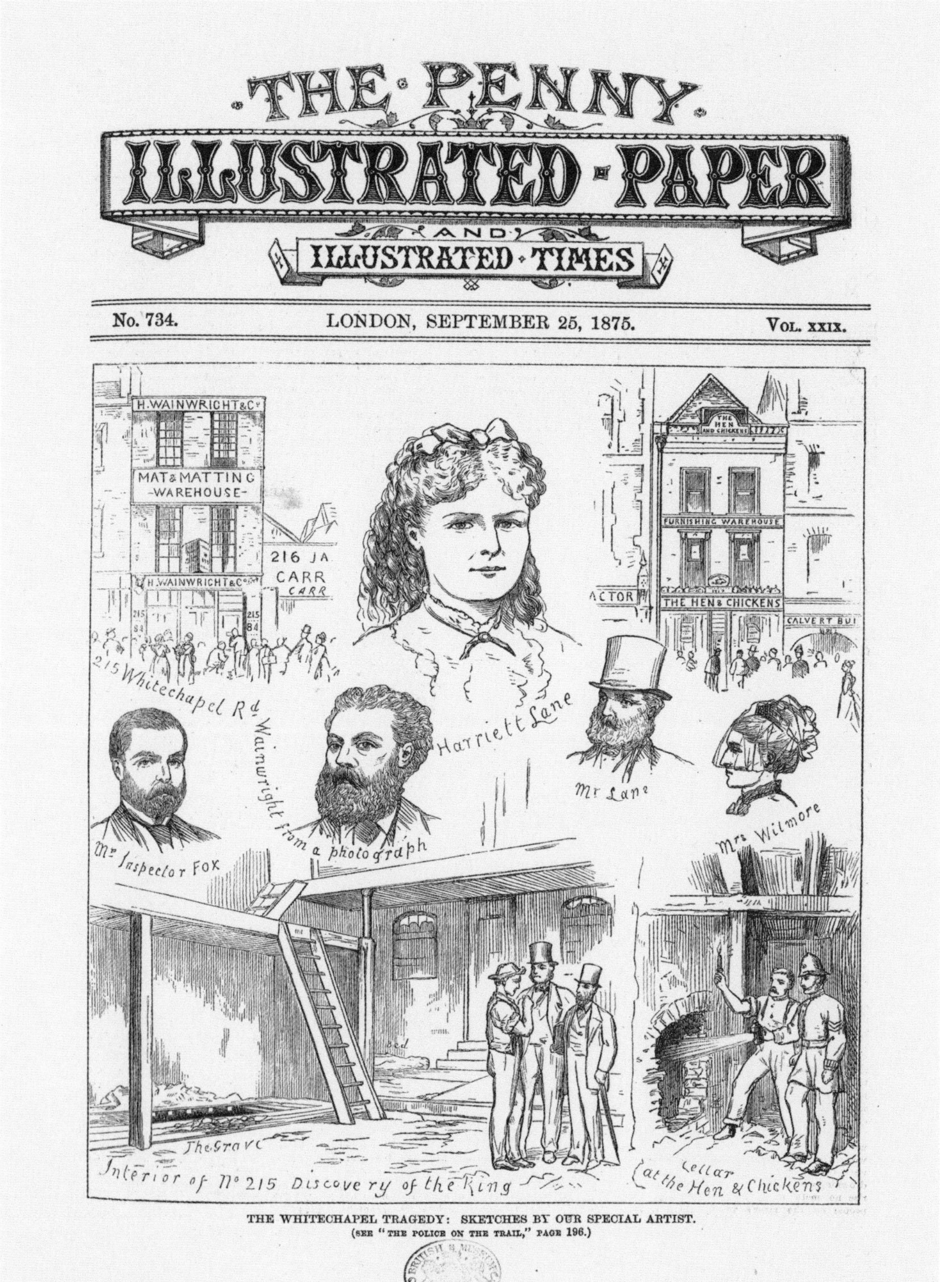

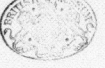

THE TOTTENHAM OUTRAGE

ANARCHISTS BRING TERROR TO EDWARDIAN LONDON

↑ A souvenir of the Tottenham Outrage with images of the characters involved, and highlighting the murder of PC Tyler.

Armed robberies were infrequent in Edwardian London and so police were rarely armed. So in 1910, when a group of politically inspired robbers snatched a payroll delivery in north London, the Met's reaction was at best haphazard. By contrast Paul Hefeld and Jacob Lepidus (Latvian refugees fleeing Tsarist persecution in Russia) had planned the heist as best they could, even if they were to lose their lives in the attempt.

Hefeld took a temporary position at the factory where the wage grab was made, and so he knew the routine and when to strike. As James Wilson, the chauffeur of the factory's owner, and the factory's office boy Albert Keyworth drove up to the gates of the Tottenham rubber works, Hefeld and Lepidus attacked. Despite brave attempts to stop them, the pair got away with about £80 in coins (about £8,000 in modern money) which they jettisoned in the chaos that followed. It was never recovered.

Hastily armed police rushed out of Tottenham station and a frantic chase forced the robbers towards open ground and the River Lea's marshland. At one point Wilson, still driving the factory car, caught them and was subjected to a barrage of small arms fire from semi-automatic weapons. He survived but a stray bullet hit a young boy named Ralph Joscelyne, fatally injuring him. PC William Tyler also became the first policeman in eight years to be killed executing his duty when he was also shot trying to run them to ground. Hefeld and Lepidus hijacked a tram only to abandon it when the conductor cleverly misled them into believing the vehicle would pass by a police station. Finally, trapped by a fence barring his way, Hefeld shot at his pursuers before turning his gun on himself; Lepidus vainly sought cover in a cottage at Hale End, but ultimately decided suicide was his best option. Police found him dead when they broke in. The Tottenham Outrage, as the papers dubbed it, was over but it was not the last that the capital was to hear about the case.

THE SIEGE OF SIDNEY STREET

CHURCHILL LOOKS ON AS A FIREFIGHT RAGES IN EAST LONDON

At 7.30 on the morning of 3 January 1911, Detective Sergeant Ben Leeson of the Metropolitan Police, lobbed a stone at the windows of 100 Sidney Street in the East End, precipitating a volley of gunfire from inside. The policeman fell to the ground, wounded. Fortunately, Leeson survived but the two gunmen inside were to die to in a conflagration that would consume their hideout and help create a lasting mythology around them.

The story of the Siege of Sidney Street began in December 1910. Police were called to Harry Harris's jewellery shop at 119 Houndsditch after neighbours heard suspicious noises emanating from inside. When police arrived, they discovered that a robbery was in progress and five officers were shot, three fatally, as the desperate burglars attempted to shoot their way out. A day later the police found one of the gunmen (George Gardstein) in Grove Street, dying of his wounds, having been shot in the crossfire at Houndsditch, most likely by his mates. Attention now focused on the remaining men, who were believed to be part of a Latvian anarchist gang supposedly (inaccurately as it turns out) led by a shadowy anti-hero named 'Peter the Painter'.

In early January, police gained intelligence which suggested the robbers had taken refuge in a house in Sidney Street in the East End. They isolated the street, forcibly evacuating the nearby houses, and laid siege. Up to one hundred police officers, supplemented by soldiers from the Scots Guards then engaged in a sustained gun battle with the fugitives which lasted for six hours, with the Home Secretary Winston Churchill apparently directing proceedings in his trademark top hat. Then, as dusk began to descend, 100 Sidney Street was set on fire, almost certainly by the police eager to bring things to a conclusion. Two charred bodies were identified as Fritz Svaars and William Sokoloff. Of Peter the Painter there was no trace.

No one was ever successfully convicted of murdering the police officers or attempting to burgle Harris's jewellers, and the myths surrounding the Siege of Sidney Street persist to this day. The case is connected to the Tottenham Outrage that had occurred two years earlier, and was a reminder that 'foreign' terrorists were still at large in the Edwardian capital.

↑ City of London wanted poster offering a reward for information leading the arrest of 'Peter the Painter'.

→ Winston Churchill, in his trademark top hat, with a group of policemen during the Siege of Sidney Street.

THE RATCLIFFE HIGHWAY MURDERS
A SERIAL KILLER MEETS A MACABRE END

In December 1811, London's East End was shocked by the brutal murder of two households in two weeks, and within a mile of each other. The slaughter of Timothy and Celia Marr and their infant son, as well as the apprentice James Gowan took place on the on 7th. This tragedy was repeated twelve days later in the killing of John Williamson, his wife Elizabeth and servant Bridget Harrington at the Williamsons' pub, the King's Arms, New Gravel Lane, where John was the landlord. John Turner narrowly escaped the carnage by knotting sheets together and climbing down from a second-floor window.

Both sets of murders had taken place on, or close to, the Ratcliffe Highway (now simply The Highway) which traversed the Wapping dockside. This area was notorious for vice and crime, with inns and brothels supplying the demands of sailors returning from long voyages with money burning holes in their pockets. Despite already being known as a disreputable area, the murders of the Marrs and Williamsons still provoked a deep sense of anxiety and anger, much of which was quickly directed at foreign sailors and the ineptitude of policing.

In 1811 London had no official police force, although the Thames River Police (created in 1800 by the magistrates Patrick Colquhoun and John Harriott) protected the interests of the merchants who traded on the river. The hunt for the Ratcliffe Highway killer fell to the local watch and Bow Street Runners (specialized thieftakers). The killer had left the murder weapons behind – a maul (a ripping chisel used in boat building) and a large hammer – but no other clues to his identity. Ratcliffe Highway also became a magnet for the curious: 'The sensation excited by these most ferocious murders has become so general, and the curiosity to see the place where they were committed so intense, that Ratcliffe Highway was rendered almost impassable by the throng of spectators before ten o'clock yesterday morning', reported *The Times* on 11 December.

The investigation, such as it was, led to the arrest of a sailor named John Williams who had loose associations with both families. It was established that he had the opportunity to steal the maul from a fellow seaman, and his landlady recalled seeing blood on his clothes. He was locked up in Coldbath Fields while enquiries continued. These were brought to a sharp halt on 28 December, however, when Williams was found dead in his cell, hanged by his own scarf.

Found guilty in absentia, his dead body was paraded along the Highway on a cart, with the maul and the hammer laid either side of him. As was customary, the cart stopped outside the King's Arms and the Marrs' home before continuing to the St George turnpike, a crossroads at the junction with what is now Commercial Road. There Williams was buried in a hastily excavated grave with a stake driven through his heart. He lay there until 1886 when gas workers, digging a trench to lay pipes around that spot, accidently unearthed his skeleton. According to legend, Williams' skull once adorned the shelves in a local pub, The Crown and Dolphin on Cannon Street Road, but of it now there is now no trace.

THE MANNINGS
A CRUEL CONSPIRACY INSPIRES A LITERARY CREATION

When Charles Dickens wrote *Bleak House* (1852–3) he based his characterisation of the maid 'Hortense', who commits a murder by shooting, on the real-life murderess Maria Manning. Manning was hanged on the roof of Horsemonger Lane Gaol on 13 November 1849 alongside her husband Frederick, for the murder of her sometime lover Patrick O'Connor.

Maria de Roux, a Swiss-born lady's maid, had met Frederick Manning while already in a relationship with O'Connor. O'Connor was a moneylender and tax collector at the docks, while Fred was a publican with a rather dubious semi-criminal past. Having picked the publican, Maria continued her dalliance with her former paramour because she thought he was a better source of money. O'Connor had shares in the railways, a boom industry in the 1840s, and Maria persuaded her husband Fred to help her murder O'Connor and steal them.

Since the Irishman was a regular visitor to the Mannings' home in Bermondsey it was easy to trick him into a fateful dinner engagement. As he washed his hands in the bathroom the pair took turns to shoot him before burying his body under the kitchen flagstones. Maria rushed to O'Connor's lodgings to steal his shares and his money. The Mannings then split up to evade police. In this they failed: Maria was hunted down in Edinburgh and Fred tracked to Jersey. Their London trial was a sensation and their execution drew one of the largest crowds of the century, including both Dickens and his literary rival Thackery.

← Maria Manning, 1849.

DANIEL GOOD
THE ESTABLISHMENT OF THE DETECTIVE DEPARTMENT

In June 1842, the commissioners of the Metropolitan Police formally established a small Detective Department. The unit had just two sergeants and six constables, but it was a start. Detection had not been part of Robert Peel's design for his 'New Police' in 1829 but it soon became apparent that detectives were necessary. In no small part this was due to the actions of Daniel Good, a thoroughly unpleasant murderer and thief.

In April 1842, police investigating the theft of a pair of trousers made a shocking discovery in the stables where Good, a coachman, worked. Good managed to trap the officers inside and escape. While they waited to be rescued, they uncovered the decomposing torso of a woman, Good's common-law wife Jane Jones. It took ten days to recapture Good, through good fortune rather than any policing skills. A retired policeman in Kent, who happened to have taken an interest in the discovery of the body because the stables were, coincidently, situated on his former beat, recognised Good. Good was taken to London and tried for the murder of Jane Jones. It took the jury just thirty-five minutes to convict him.

He went to the gallows outside Newgate Prison on 23 May 1842, loudly protesting his innocence. The executioner Calcraft despatched him quickly in front of a near-record crowd of spectators. Soon after the Detective Department was set up so that future efforts to catch notorious criminals were predicated on detection, rather than reliant on chance.

↑ Daniel Good at Bow Street Police Court.

CHARLES PEACE

THE MOST NOTORIOUS CRIMINAL OF THE NINETEENTH CENTURY

By all accounts Charles Peace was a deeply unattractive man. Physically damaged from a series of accidents in his youth, and morally bankrupt, Peace turned to crime in his teens, serving several terms of imprisonment. It could have been so different, as Peace was very talented; a musician and entertainer, craftsman and inventor, able to alter his appearance like an actor, and not without charm – as his womanising suggests.

Moreover, if Peace had stuck to burglary, which he was extremely adept at, then prison or transportation to Australia might have been the worst of his fate. As it was, in 1876, aged forty-four, he killed a jealous husband (Arthur Dyson) and this changed everything. Having burgled his way from Yorkshire to Peckham in London, Peace was captured after a tussle with two policemen who had interrupted a burglary. Peace shot one of the officers and, using the pseudonym 'Ward', was tried and found guilty of attempted murder. When he was sentenced to life imprisonment and sent to Pentonville, his real identity was revealed. Wanted for the murder of Dyson in Leeds, he was transferred back there to face trial.

The jury needed just fifteen minutes to convict Peace of murder and the judge passed sentence of death upon him. In Armley Prison, Peace confessed his crimes, including the murder of a police officer in Manchester, and wrote his memoirs. He went bravely to the gallows, according to his executioner Marwood, earning the sobriquet of the 'most notorious criminal of the nineteenth century'.

← A scene from the life of Charles Peace. Peace is seated on the left.

→ Detectives working undercover as dockers pose for a photograph, c. 1911.

THE SPITALFIELDS WEAVERS
ANGER AND TRAGEDY AS PASSIONS RUN HIGH

On a bitterly cold April day in 1771, Daniel Clarke, a middle-aged silk pattern maker, ran for his life from an angry mob. Clarke had been identified as someone whose evidence had led directly to the public execution of William Eastman, one of five individuals held responsible for the breaking of silk weaving frames.

The frames were owned by Lewis Chauvet, one of the most prominent weaving masters in Spitalfields, with whom weavers were in a long-running pay dispute. Chauvet bribed witnesses to testify against the weavers, two of whom had been hanged in a chaotic execution at Bethnal Green, near the scene of the crime. This provoked a crowd into an act of defiance, tearing down the gallows and rebuilding them outside Chauvet's workshop.

Clarke was no innocent but he didn't deserve the summary justice now meted out to him. Discovered hiding in the home of a friend, he was chased across Spitalfields to a large pond. There the mob forced him into the freezing water and pelted him with stones and bricks until he collapsed and drowned.

Injustice now piled on to the tragedy as three people were arrested and tried for this murder. One of these, Henry Stroud, had seemingly tried to intervene to save him. It made no difference in court, especially when witnesses were again bribed to testify against him. Stroud and another man, Robert Campbell (who was more actively involved in Clarke's murder) were publicly hanged at Bethnal Green on a scaffold erected specially for the occasion.

SHOOTING OF SPENCER PERCEVAL
THE ONLY BRITISH PM TO BE ASSASSINATED

Only one British Prime Minister has been assassinated, and Spencer Perceval will forever be remembered for that unwelcome accolade. Perceval served as the Tory MP for Northampton from 1796. His political rise was meteoric, his legal background helping him assume the roles of Solicitor General and Attorney General, before being appointed Chancellor of the Exchequer in 1807. Two years later he was Prime Minister, nine years after entering politics.

It was his time as Chancellor that caused his death. In 1804 John Bellingham was imprisoned for debt in Russia for five years. When he returned to England, he turned his anger on Perceval's Treasury for failing to support him. He bought a brace of pistols and began to practise shooting.

On 11 May 1812, he calmly strode up to Perceval in the lobby of the House of Commons and shot him. Struck in the chest Perceval cried out 'I am murdered!' before collapsing at the feet of the MP for Norfolk. As the fatally wounded Perceval was carried away, Bellingham simply sat down on a nearby bench. He is reported as saying, 'I have been ill-treated . . . I have sought redress in vain. I am a most unfortunate man and feel sufficient justification for what I have done'.

A quick trial at the Old Bailey followed, with the inevitable result that Bellingham was hanged outside Newgate Prison on 18 May. Troops were carefully positioned to watch the crowd amid fears (unfounded it seems) that his action was not single-minded but, in some way, revolutionary.

← Bellingham shoots the Prime Minister.

←← Silk weaving in Spitalfields.

PENTONVILLE AND LONDON'S PRISON SYSTEM

A LEGACY THAT ENDURES TO THIS DAY

We are so used to the idea of prison as a punishment that it is easy to forget that until the late 1700s prisons were mostly used to house offenders awaiting trial, those about to be executed or transported, or for individuals who had been imprisoned for debt (**see page 181**). Imprisonment was not routinely used then, as a punishment, and certainly not for the rehabilitation of offenders.

England's first 'national' prison was built in 1819 on the banks of the Thames at Millbank (where the Tate Modern art gallery now stands), but it was Pentonville, which opened in 1842, that established the idea of imprisonment as the state's main form of punishment. Pentonville functioned as a part of a growing carceral landscape of institutions that included Brixton (originally a women's prison), Parkhurst on the Isle of Wight (for juveniles), Portland and Portsmouth (where prisoners engaged in public works) and Broadmoor (for the criminally insane).

Pentonville was established to deliver the 'separate' system – one of two competing ideas for treating convicts. Under the alternative 'silent' system, prisoners were allowed to associate with each other but not speak. Under the separate system they were to be kept apart and isolated for almost the entirety of their sentence. This was enforced in a variety of ways. Prisoners had single cells and the prison chapel was fitted with box-like spaces so prisoners could only see the chaplain. Work and exercise were conducted wearing masks, so identities were concealed and the sense of exclusion maintained.

The purpose of all this was to inculcate change from within, inspiring a 'crisis of conscience' that would reform offenders. This was supported by forms of hard labour which included such pointless exercises as turning the crank handle, or climbing for hours on a treadwheel. The Victorians believed they could 'grind men good' in prison, and so a system that by the 1870s was described as 'hard labour, hard bed, hard fare', ensured that anyone thinking that imprisonment might be preferable to the workhouse would quickly realise their mistake.

Reformation and rehabilitation were certainly in the minds of prison reformers like Jeremy Bentham and John Howard in the late 1700s but a lack of money coupled with the negative public opinion of criminals meant that as Britain entered the twentieth century her prisons were dreadful places where inmates were crushed, both physically and mentally, rather than being healed and reformed. The Victorian systems were soon abandoned after the First World War, when significant numbers of 'respectable', often middle-class prisoners (Suffragettes housed in Holloway and numerous male conscientious objectors), reported back on their experience. What did not disappear overnight was the physical structure of prisons, and any visitor to (or inmate of) several of London's existing prisons, most notably Wandsworth in the south, will recognise that we still house modern prisoners in Victorian buildings.

↑ A prisoner turns the crank in his cell, a monotonous task that was supposed to focus the convict's mind on reformation.

THE MURDER OF WILLIAM TERRISS
A THESPIAN FACES HIS FINAL ACT

↑ William Terriss, on the left, performing in *The Fatal Card*, an 1880s melodrama.

→→ Prisoners wash at low basins with officers observing onboard the convict hulk ship, the Warrior.

William Terriss and Richard Prince were jobbing stage actors. Terriss was quite well known in the 1890s, and considered to be one of the best of the period, Prince perhaps less so. Unsurprisingly then there was rivalry, and no little jealousy on Prince's part.

On the evening of 16 December 1897, Terriss shared a taxi to the Adelphi Theatre in Covent Garden with his close friend John Henry Graves, arriving at the stage door just after 7 p.m. As Terriss went to open the door Prince rushed over from the other side of the street and attacked him with a knife. Terriss was stabbed twice in the back and collapsed in Graves's arms. His friend seized the assailant and held him till a policeman answered his cries of 'Murder!' Terriss died soon afterwards, cradled in the bosom of his sweetheart, Jessie Millward, herself an actress.

Around 50,000 theatre folk and fans turned out for Terriss' funeral at Brompton Cemetery, where the famous actor Henry Irving read a message of sympathy from Queen Victoria. Richard Archer (Prince was a stage name) was found guilty but, as several medical witnesses were able to attest to his poor mental state, was deemed not responsible for his actions. The judge sent him to Holloway to await Her Majesty's pleasure. He was finally sent to Broadmoor Prison for the Criminally Insane, and detained as a 'criminal lunatic' until his death in 1937. There is a rumour that Terriss' ghost haunts the Covent Garden underground station, and the Adelphi, with sightings reported as recently as 2008.

PRISON HULKS
SEMINARIES OF PROFLIGACY AND VICE

From 1718, legislation allowed judges to send England's unwanted felons over the seas to plantations in colonial America. This came to a crushing halt in 1775 when unhappy colonists rebelled against direct rule and the American War of Independence (1775–1783) began. The British government didn't anticipate the hiatus to be anything other than temporary, and so an interim means of dealing with convicts was found.

A law was passed allowing those sentenced to transportation to be held on a floating prison hulk and set to hard labour improving defences for the war effort. The hulks, decommissioned naval ships, were awful: men died of disease (typhus and dysentery) or in conditions worse than any of the capital's prisons. Men worked ten hours a day in good weather, seven in the winter. Those not labouring were locked up below. The Justitia hulk had space for 125 convicts but by 1779 held 250, and the Censor was designed for 183 but housed 256. Hulks were training grounds for criminals ('seminaries of profligacy and vice' one magistrate dubbed them) – no reformation was taking place.

Transportation restarted in 1787 (to New South Wales) but the use of the hulks continued, with additional decommissioned naval vessels at Deptford, Plymouth and Portsmouth housing young offenders and prisoners of war. In 1847 an exposé of conditions prompted improvements but prisoners still rebelled against their treatment. The experiment with floating prisons was abandoned in 1857 when the Defence, the last remaining hulk on the Thames, was set ablaze and destroyed.

↑ Convicts from hulks anchored in the Thames near Woolwich set to work on the riverbank.

DR CRIPPEN

A KILLER CAUGHT BY TELEGRAPHY

'Doctor' Hawley Harvey Crippen is often credited with the most sensational murder of Edwardian London. In response to concerns raised by friends of Crippen's wife Cora, Chief Inspector Walter Dew began an investigation into her disappearance from 39 Hilldrop Crescent, Holloway. Cora Crippen (aka Belle Elmore) was a colourful stage personality and her relationship with Hawley was tempestuous.

At some point Crippen began an affair with his secretary Ethel Le Neve and in January 1910 Cora vanished. Crippen explained that she had gone abroad, then revealed she'd died of an illness. Under Dew's questioning Crippen admitted his infidelity with Le Neve and confessed to lying about Cora's death. His new story was that she'd deserted him. When Dew returned days later he found 39 Hilldrop Crescent deserted: Crippen and Le Neve had fled. A search of the house unearthed human remains under the flagstones. 'The head was missing', Dew later wrote, and so 'identification seemed impossible'. Nevertheless, skilled forensics experts were sure that this was Cora's mutilated body.

Crippen appeared to have poisoned her with hyoscine, an unusual means of killing. Crippen had some medical training, and he'd recently bought 5 grains of hyoscine hydrobromide. Armed with proof of Crippen's guilt this is where the story became an international sensation. Captain Kendall of the *Montrose*, a passenger ship sailing to Canada, read press reports of Crippen's flight

and realised Crippen and Le Neve (posing as a boy) were onboard. He wired his office, they alerted Dew, and the detective boarded a faster vessel which arrived ahead of the *Montrose*. Dew went aboard disguised as a ship's pilot, and made the arrest on 21 July. Crippen appeared almost relieved to be arrested, and made no attempt to escape.

It took several more months before they were returned to England and put on trial in October. Crippen and Le Neve's trial lasted four days but it took the jury just twenty-seven minutes to return a verdict. Crippen was convicted of murder while Ethel was acquitted of being an accessory, and she later sold her story. John Ellis hanged Crippen at Pentonville prison on 23 November 1910. This was the first time that a criminal had been effectively tracked down using wireless telegraphy. 39 Hilldrop Crescent, which was close to the prison at Holloway, no longer exists, having been demolished in 1951.

Cora Crippen's head has never been found so it remains possible, if unlikely, that Crippen did not murder her. Indeed, it has been suggested, but refuted, that Dew or his colleagues planted evidence to incriminate Hawley Crippen. As a junior detective in the Whitechapel Murders case (**see page 30**) Dew may have felt he could not have two unsolved high-profile murders on his caseload.

↑ Cora Crippen, aka Belle Elmore (left), and Crippen and Ethel Le Neve in the dock at Bow Street Police Court (right).

CRIME & PUNISHMENT

DUELLING IN LONDON — PISTOLS AT DAWN

One of the most evocative images of Georgian England is two men duelling over a slight to their honour. Open spaces such as Hampstead Heath, Chalk Farm and Wandsworth and Wimbledon Commons were all favourite sites for duelling. The classic fencing match gave way to 'pistols at dawn' because swordsmanship was a highly skilled activity most often the preserve of the elite, while the pistol was much easier to use.

The wearing of swords declined from the 1720s, and so from 1793 seconds (representatives for each party) would arrange duels with pistols. Pistols were inaccurate, levelling the playing field and meaning that there was an element of chance not present in swordfights. Men duelled with pistols at ten or twelve paces; any closer and the chances of fatalities increased, while any further risked making a mockery of the occasion.

Many duellists were military men, despite attempts to prohibit this in the army, but by the 1820s the respectable 'middling sorts', seeing duelling as a way to assert their social status, dominated. This, along with prosecutions for homicide, contributed to duelling's decline.

The Duke of Wellington fought a duel with Lord Winchilsea on Battersea Fields in 1829, wounding him in the leg. In 1840, Lord Cardigan (of Light Brigade fame) was charged with wounding a former dragoon, but got off on a technicality. The very last duel in London was fought between Lieutenant-Colonel David Fawcett and Lieutenant Alexander Monroe. Fawcett, reportedly shot in the abdomen, died later that night in the nearby Camden Town tavern.

↑ A classic pistol duel at dawn.

ASSASSINATION ATTEMPTS ON QUEEN VICTORIA
TAKING POTSHOTS AT HER MAJESTY

Queen Victoria might have been one of England's longest-reigning monarchs (eclipsed only by Elizabeth II) but she was far from the most popular. She was a young and unexpected occupant of the throne in 1837, considered easily influenced by Lord Melbourne, her first Prime Minister. Nor was her choice of husband welcomed; Prince Albert of Saxe-Coburg and Gotha was a reminder of the German (Hanoverian) rulers people were keen to see the back of. That said, it is still something of a surprise to learn she survived no fewer than eight attempts on her life.

The first was in June 1840, when Edward Oxford, a 'slightly made youth of eighteen' shot at her moving carriage as it made its way along Constitution Hill. Oxford was confined in Bedlam asylum. Following the second attempt, in 1842, John Francis (aged nineteen) was tried for treason, convicted and set to hang before being reprieved and exiled to Australia. John William Bean's attempt, also in 1842, almost passed unnoticed as the diminutive assassin's gun failed to go off as the Queen's carriage passed by. He was picked up at midnight following his identification by police.

The next assassination attempt took place in 1849. William Hamilton was an Irishman radicalised by revolutionary fervour experienced in Paris. He took a potshot at

→ Roderick Maclean shoots at the Queen's carriage in 1882.

Victoria on Constitution Hill, but failed to harm her. Hamilton was sentenced to seven years' transportation. A 'dandy' named Robert Pate did manage to injure the Queen. He strode up to her carriage in June 1850 and struck her with his cane before being quickly subdued by the crowd. Pate pleaded not guilty to two counts of having an offensive weapon with intent to cause harm, and was convicted and sentenced to seven years' transportation.

Victoria's life was untroubled by assassins for twenty-seven years, but she lost Albert and almost lost her eldest son. Having returned from a service at St Paul's to give thanks for the Prince of Wales' recovery from illness, Arthur O'Connor made the most audacious attempt on her life yet. With a gun concealed in his pocket he climbed the railings surrounding Buckingham Palace. Fortunately for Victoria, he was overwhelmed moments later as he confronted her. He may have been motivated by the cause of Irish republicanism, but his gun wasn't loaded and he was clearly not entirely sane. He got a short spell in prison and a flogging, something Victoria had personally insisted not be applied to earlier would-be assassins.

In 1882, Roderick Maclean, a 'disaffected artist', bought a gun and hiked fifty-seven miles from Southsea to Windsor, where on 2 March, as the Queen returned by train from London, he shot at her carriage. Maclean was overpowered by two Eton schoolboys. Initially he was found not guilty by reason of insanity, but Victoria's anger at this led to a legal change that enabled Maclean to be found 'guilty, but insane'. He was sent to Broadmoor. The final attempt on Victoria's life was arguably the most serious, in that it was planned as part of an Irish republican ('Fenian') terror wave that washed over Britain in the 1880s (**see page 34**), with an abortive attempt to blow up Westminster Abbey as the Queen celebrated her Golden Jubilee.

BRIXTON BABY FARMERS

CRUELTY TO CHILDREN
STUPEFIED BY LAUDANUM

On 11 October 1870, Margaret Waters was hanged inside Horsemonger Lane Gaol for the murder of the infant John Walter Cowen. Waters was charged with the murder of four more infants, and suspected of being responsible for the deaths of as many as nineteen. Her sister Sarah Ellis was accused of being an accessory and of taking money by false pretences. Ellis would go to prison for eighteen months.

There were many 'baby farmers' in the 1800s, but Waters was one of the most notorious. Baby farming was a form of unregulated fostering, and open to abuse. Mothers placed their illegitimate children with a baby farmer to raise, paying a weekly fee for their care. Often the money was insufficient and some baby farmers struggled to look after the children adequately. Consequently, many infants died of unintentional neglect.

Waters deliberately engineered the death of the babies in her care. She plied them with opiates, suppressing their appetites, and, when they died of malnourishment, wrapped them in brown paper and dumped their bodies in the streets. When police arrived at her home they found '[s]ome half-dozen little infants [lying] together on a sofa, filthy, starving, and stupefied by laudanum'. The scandal caused by the case prompted the passing of the Infant Life Protection Act (1872) which gave local authorities the power to enforce the registration of those taking in children under five, and so protect them against callous baby farmers like Waters.

→ The execution of Margaret Waters.

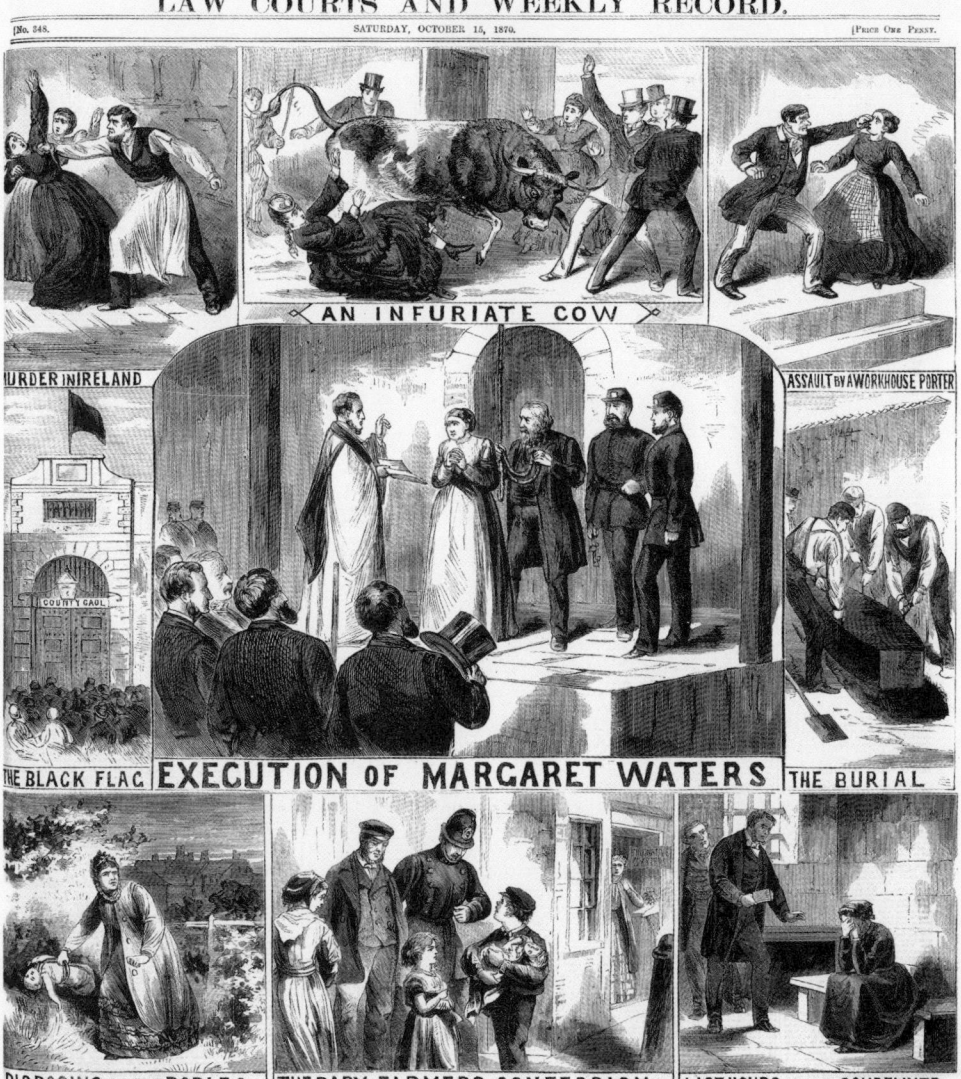

FLORENCE BRAVO

DID SHE KILL HER HUSBAND?

When Florence Bravo's first husband, the abusive alcoholic Alexander Ricardo, died after a drinking bout in Germany, he left her a young widow with a fortune of £7,000 a year (roughly £680,000 today). Florence had been receiving medical treatment throughout her short marriage and it seems she formed a relationship with her physician, Dr Gully despite him being much older. Florence was encouraged to remarry, in part to quell the rumours about Gully. Her 'companion' Jane Cox helped find an eligible partner, Charles Bravo, who she married in December 1875.

The honeymoon period didn't last long and Florence found herself embroiled in another unsatisfactory relationship. Then in April 1876 Charles Bravo fell ill and mysteriously died. Poison was detected and the finger of accusation pointed at Florence and Cox. However, the coroner's inquest concluded Bravo may have taken his own life by ingesting tartar emetic, a poison derived from antimony, and declared an open verdict. This outraged Bravo's friends and family and a criminal investigation began. Florence offered a reward of £500 for information as to how antimony had entered the Bravo household.

A second inquest convened and Florence's affair with Dr Gully was put forward as a motive for the murder. In the end there was simply insufficient proof of foul play and the jury declared Bravo's death accidental. Florence may have been exonerated but public opinion deemed her culpable. With her reputation in tatters she died just two years later, somewhat ironically, of alcoholism.

THE GORDON RIOTS
A WEEK OF CHAOS IN HANOVERIAN LONDON

↑ Lord George Gordon, whose actions provoked a week of rioting in London.

← Florence Bravo is examined at the coroner's inquest.

On Friday 2 June 1780, Lord George Gordon addressed a crowd of 50,000 at St George's Fields, across the Thames from Parliament. Gordon and his followers opposed the lifting of restrictions that prevented Catholics from undertaking public service, most importantly serving in the army. He presented a petition of 44,000 signatures for consideration by the assembled politicians. Parliament debated this for six hours but postponed judgment until the following Tuesday.

The frustrations of the crowd gathered outside now erupted into a week of rioting. Protesters ran amok, targeting the homes and businesses of Catholics and, as authorities tried to quell the disturbances, turned their anger on magistrates and the justice system. Newgate and other prisons were burned to the ground, as rioters sought to free those arrested. On 'Black Wednesday' (7 June 1780) the Bank of England was attacked; George III declared martial law and brought troops onto the streets. Hundreds were killed or wounded and dozens more were arrested, tried, and executed for their part in the violence.

Gordon was locked up, tried and acquitted of orchestrating the riots, having disassociated himself from them. The riots revealed the problems of having no centrally organised system of police, but nothing would change fundamentally for fifty years. Nor were the rioters successful in trying to overturn the 1778 Catholic Relief Act, although fear of 'popery' probably increased and the actions of the government did nothing to quell concerns about the growth of a 'big state'.

THE MCDANIEL GANG
THIEF-TAKING AND A BLOOD-MONEY SCANDAL

↑ Stephen McDaniel, the eponymous leader of a notorious gang of thief-takers.

In 1692 Queen Anne's government created legislation which offered rewards for the successful prosecution of highwaymen, in response to concerns about rising crime. The scheme was extended to crimes such as shoplifting, burglary and counterfeiting. As an incentive for ensuring criminals were caught, tried, and punished, rewards of £40 (perhaps as much as £7,250 now) plus property (the highwayman's horse and weapons for example) could be handed over.

The scheme created entrepreneurial thief-takers: groups of men who made it their business (literally) to investigate crimes and pursue criminals. As we might imagine this was open to corruption and in 1725 the most notorious of these crime fighters – Jonathan Wild, self-styled 'Thief-taker General', was hanged for his abuse of the system. He was not alone and many individuals profited from the 'blood money' available for prosecuting crimes which frequently resulted in offenders (often duped into criminal activity) being sent to the gallows or transported.

In 1754, a scandal involving Stephen McDaniel and John Berry and their 'McDaniel Gang' members undermined a trial of robbers at Maidstone in Kent when it was revealed that they had been the victims of a conspiracy. The robbery they were accused of had been staged so that Berry and McDaniel and their co-conspirators could bag the £40 reward plus add-ons. They stood to get away with £120 (£21,600); instead they were convicted of conspiracy and murder and sentenced to death. They escaped the noose however, and instead were set in the pillory (**see page 17**) to face the wrath of the crowd.

NEWGATE PRISON

LONDON'S BASTILLE

There had been a goal of sorts on the site for 900 years by the time Newgate Prison was finally demolished to make way for the Central Criminal Court on Old Bailey in 1903. Newgate was invariably an old, overcrowded and insanitary prison which housed individuals awaiting their trials, convicted felons waiting to be executed or transported, and debtors waiting (or forlornly hoping) for their luck to change.

Newgate burned down in 1666 during the Great Fire, was rebuilt by Christopher Wren before being redesigned and enlarged in 1769, on a design created by George Dance (the Younger). Dance's construction was deliberately grim and foreboding, intended to serve as a visual deterrent to criminality. The Gordon Rioters (**see page 65**) didn't seem much deterred however, engulfing the gaol in flames in 1780 and releasing its prisoners. Dance was recalled to repair the damage and the redesigned prison reopened in 1782 at a cost to the City of around £4.5 million at today's prices.

Newgate was never intended to reform offenders and remained throughout the 1800s as something of an anachronism, as model prisons like Pentonville (**see page 50**) were created. Prison reformer Elizabeth Fry was a regular visitor to the female prisoners at Newgate in the early 1800s, offering support and religious teachings. Also, infamously, Newgate was where public executions took place in London after Tyburn gallows was abandoned in 1783. The last execution outside Newgate's gates took place on 26 May 1868 when Michael Barrett was hanged for his part in the bombing of Clerkenwell Prison.

← A prisoner awaits his fate in the condemned cell while a warder keeps watch over him.

← The imposing, exterior view of Newgate Prison, 1800.

CRIME & PUNISHMENT 69

HOUSES OF CORRECTION
A SHORT, SHARP SHOCK FOR THE CAPITAL'S NE'ER-DO-WELLS

London's houses of correction (or 'correctional prisons' as the contemporary commentator Henry Mayhew termed them) differed from convict prisons like Pentonville (**see page 50**) in a number of ways. First, they were run by the local magistracy, not by Her Majesty's directorate of prisons. Second, and perhaps most importantly, they were designed to house those convicted of lesser offences carrying shorter terms of imprisonment, typically a week to three years. Finally, those sent there were set to work as a punishment, generally by means of 'an apparatus designed to carry out the sentence of hard labour by rendering the work as irksome as possible'.

London had four 'correctional prisons' in the mid-nineteenth century, one in the City at Holloway, one at Wandsworth in Surrey, and two in Middlesex (Coldbath Fields and Tothill Fields). Coldbath Fields in Clerkenwell catered for adult males while women and juvenile offenders went to Tothill Fields, close to the national prison of Millbank by the River Thames. Inmates at Coldbath Fields could expect to spend their days on the treadwheel, climbing as much as 7,200 feet over four and half hours (for reference Ben Nevis, Britain's highest mountain is a mere 4,413 feet). The crank was also used as hard labour, where the turnkeys (gaolers) could set the resistance of the handle by adjusting a screw.

At Tothill Fields those who failed to obey the strict rules of the gaol were locked in the 'darks', deprived not only of company but also of any light or sound. This extreme form of solitary confinement was a popular way for prison staff to break inmates' resolve and maintain discipline. Juvenile offenders, mostly boys, would be set to work picking oakum, a monotonous and painful exercise involving separating the fibres of ropes used by the Navy, a task also assigned to many in workhouses across London.

At Wandsworth the separate system was enforced (**see page 50**). At Holloway the women were also sat in stalls to pick oakum, so they too were unable to communicate with each other. Hard labour in a London house of correction was a severe sentence even if it was not always a very long one, and Mayhew's reportage makes it clear this was something which offenders were keen to avoid. Sadly, for them, there was no escaping it if a magistrate or judge passed sentence upon them.

LOMBARD STREET BULLION ROBBERY

AN INSIDE JOB?

Readers might be familiar with the audacious Hatton Garden diamond heist of 2016 and the Great Train Robbery of 1963. Less well known, but of equal notoriety, was a gold bullion robbery in Lombard Street in 1864. On the morning of 6 December that year the London press reported the discovery of a break-in at 58 Lombard Street, City of London, the premises of Frederick Baum, a well-established City trader.

Somehow thieves accessed the safe and it was initially believed that they had stolen coins, banknotes and bills of exchange valued at about £25,000 (or £2,684,000 at modern values). They managed to subdue the Baum's large and ferocious guard dog but, thankfully, had not otherwise harmed it. Baum issued a reward of £500 and the press speculated that the robbers may have had inside knowledge, or had secreted themselves in the property overnight, giving themselves a weekend to expedite the theft.

The City of London detective unit was tasked with tracing the missing 'treasure' which Mr Baum was at pains to declare was much less in value than had been suggested. While arrests

were made and several individuals brought before the Mansion House magistrates, no one was ever charged in connection with the raid. Even if the value of the robbery was downgraded to somewhere closer to £5–10,000 (£500,000–£1,000,000 today) this was still a huge sum of money in the 1860s, equivalent to several lifetimes of work for the average skilled tradesman.

↑ A scene in a counting house.

←← Juvenile prisoners exercising at Tothill Fields.

CRIME & PUNISHMENT 71

MARY PEARCEY AND THE HAMPSTEAD TRAGEDY

COULD JACK THE RIPPER HAVE BEEN A WOMAN?

At 7 p.m. on 24 October 1890 a man discovered the body of a dead woman on Crossfield Road, Belsize Park. The victim was Phoebe Hogg and the post-mortem revealed that her skull was smashed in and her throat cut so badly that her head was almost severed from her body. Soon afterwards an abandoned pram was found in Hamilton Terrace covered in blood. Inside, the body of an infant female was found; she (Tiggy) had been suffocated.

As news of the murder spread, Phoebe's husband Frank Hogg arrived at the local police station and reported that his wife and child were missing. Suspicion soon fell on Mary Pearcey, as she had been seen wheeling the Hoggs' pram earlier that evening. Police went to her home and found blood everywhere, including on an apron and a large kitchen knife, which Mary (who sat calmly playing the piano while the police search unfolded) attributed to her attempts to deal with vermin. Her strange behaviour was now compounded by her singing 'killing mice, killing, killing mice' in response to police questioning.

Pearcey was tried and convicted of murder and hanged on 23 December 1890 by the executioner James Berry. Madame Tussauds Waxworks managed to purchase the pram and much of the furniture and chattels from Pearcey's kitchen to fashion its tableau of the murderer. In 1939 William Stewart named Pearcey as a suspect in the Jack the Ripper (Whitechapel) murder case.

→ Mary Pearcey and her mother at Holloway jail.

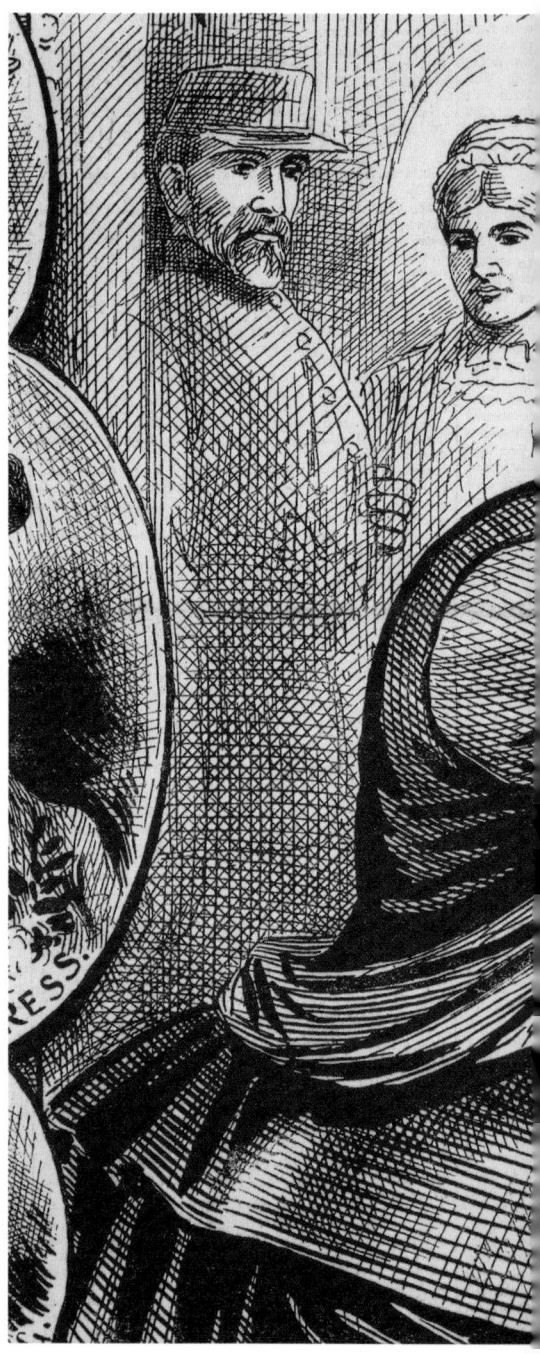

DEATH & THE SUPERNATURAL

BUNHILL FIELDS

A RESTING PLACE FOR LONDON'S NONCONFORMISTS

Nestling by the busy City Road lies Bunhill ('Bone Hill') Fields Burial Ground. Burials took place here from 1665, in response to the plague which devasted London in the year before the Great Fire. Bunhill Fields became the last resting place of 120,000 Londoners, many of whom were Nonconformists (non-Anglican worshippers such as Wesleyans, Quakers, but also Catholics and Jews). Among the most famous of these are the visionary poet William Blake, John Bunyan (author of *Pilgrim's Progress*), Thomas Fowell Buxton, an anti-slavery campaigner, and Daniel Defoe, the celebrated author of *Robinson Crusoe*.

Less well known is Dame Mary Page whose funerary monument records that: 'In 67 months she was tap'd 66 times, had taken away 240 gallons [over 1,000 litres] of water'. Mary died of dropsy (oedema/edema today) where the area under the skin fills with fluid, so the treatment was to be pricked and drained.

In the 1700s, Bunhill became a target for graverobbers keen to profit from the need for cadavers (**see page 110**). In 1852, Parliament legislated to close burial grounds which were deemed to be 'full', and attention was directed towards finding larger spaces on the peripheries of the metropolis to bury the dead. This initiated the laying out of seven 'magnificent' new cemeteries (**see page 82**) to cater for London's growing population. Bunhill Fields was closed to burials after 1854 (Elizabeth Howell Oliver was the final internment), becoming a public space in 1869.

↑ An evocative drawing of Bunhill Fields, which has not changed much in 100 years.

SARAH WHITEHEAD

THE NUN WHO HAUNTS THE BANK OF ENGLAND

MISS WHITEHEAD.
The Bank Nun.

↑ Sarah Whitehead was a frequent visitor to Threadneedle Street and her ghost is said to haunt the Bank of England to this day.

Paul Whitehead was a Bank of England clerk. Sadly, Whitehead was altogether too fond of the finer things of life, or, as a contemporary noted, 'rather too high-minded for his income'. Living beyond his means led him to run up debts and, as his creditors closed in, he decided to take advantage of his employment to repay them. It was a fatal mistake.

In October 1811 he was charged with forging a bill of exchange (a document authorising a money transfer) for £87 (£6,000 at today's prices). He was tried and convicted at the Old Bailey and executed outside Newgate Prison on 26 January 1812. Whitehead's sister Sarah was unmarried and devoted to her brother. She was unaware of her brother's fall from grace until she went to look for him at the Bank where she learned of his death from a clerk.

The shock sent her mad and, unable to process this devasting news, she started calling at the bank to ask after him. Dressed in black crepe, synonymous with mourning, she became a familiar sight on Threadneedle Street, where the local traders took pity on her, buying her food or a glass of brandy. She became known as the 'Bank Nun', and returned every working day until 1818 when the Bank's directors offered her money to stop. There is no record of what happened to Sarah but she became the subject of a penny fiction novella, *The Lady in Black*, and her ghost is said to haunt the Bank of England to this day.

DEATH & THE SUPERNATURAL

THE HAMMERSMITH GHOST
A FATAL CASE OF MISTAKEN IDENTITY

During the winter of 1803–4 the residents of Hammersmith, west London, were disturbed by sightings of a spectral figure, clad in white cloth, which haunted the district. It was widely believed to be the ghost of a local man who'd taken his own life a few years earlier. Rumours spread easily in the dark nights of winter as locals supped ale and told tall stories by parlour fireplaces.

William Girdler, a local watchman (a form of early policeman), testified that 'many people were very much frightened' by the apparition, and some of the braver souls determined to do something about it. Patrols went out every night looking for the ghost, and, perhaps inevitably, they saw what they expected to see.

A local bricklayer named Thomas Milward had a habit of dressing in white clothes. Milward once drew the attention of the occupants of a passing carriage who shouted, 'here goes the ghost!' which Milward met with insults and threats of violence. Despite the pleas of his mother-in-law Milward continued to dress in white which made him a target for ghost hunters. A nervous Francis Smith mistook him for the Hammersmith ghost and shot him dead. Smith surrendered to the authorities on discovering his mistake, and was convicted at the Old Bailey on 11 January. He was saved from the rope by the king's pardon, and was sent to prison where he remained until July 1804. Of the actual ghost no trace was ever found.

← A contemporary (and heavily stylised) engraving of the Hammersmith ghost from the magazine *Kirby's Wonderful and Scientific Museum*, 1804.

→ Francis Smith mistakes Thomas Milward for the Hammersmith ghost!

THE CHELSEA GHOST
THE HAUNTING THAT WASN'T

Empty properties were often associated with hauntings (**see page 94**). Often there was little or no truth in the stories, but strange sounds and unexplained sightings can prompt local speculation especially if a building was being used as a temporary shelter, or a place for children to act out their fantasies. This was the case with 49 Halsey Street, Chelsea in 1882.

That summer the house's owner disappeared without leaving a forwarding address. As the autumn nights drew in, school children dared themselves to sneak glimpses through the darkened windows, or to knock on the door and run away. They soon convinced themselves the place was haunted. As a result, 49 Halsey Street became a target and its windows were smashed, the door beaten, and bells rung to frighten the spectre away.

Things came to a head on 16 October when Eliza Sims, fortified by a considerable amount of 'Dutch courage' approached the property and banged loudly on the door. A crowd gathered shouting encouragement as the drunken woman repeatedly struck at the portal demanding that 'the ghost' surrender and vacate the house.

The presence of a 'large and turbulent mob' (as the papers described it) attracted the police who arrested Eliza for being drunk and disorderly. Sometime later the door of the house opened and a figure, clad in white with a very tall white hat emerged, brandishing a cudgel. But it wasn't a ghost at all, it was a sixteen-year-old errand boy named William Dakin, who was promptly arrested.

← William Dakin has his collar felt by the long arm of the law.

COUNT CAGLIOSTRO
THE SELF-DUBBED COUNT FROM GOD KNOWS WHERE

In July 1776 Count Alessandro di Cagliostro (aka Giuseppe Balsamo) took rooms in Whitcomb Street, near London's fashionable Pall Mall, with his wife, the exotic Lorenza Seraphina Feliciani who'd run away with him when she was just fourteen. Cagliostro was a fascinating member of European Enlightenment society. A gifted forger (he once impersonated Casanova in a letter), and a teller of tall tales, he ranged across the European continent from the late 1760s to his death in prison in 1795.

He lived in London sporadically throughout the 1770s and 80s, and helped establish Freemason lodges here and abroad. James Gillray, one of the most talented satirical cartoonists of the period, sketched a satire on Cagliostro in 1786, ridiculing him as 'a self-dubbed count' from 'god knows where'. Gillray reflected contemporary scepticism of Cagliostro and his dubious character. For a time, he was imprisoned in the Bastille in Paris, accused of stealing a necklace of Marie Antoinette's, but was released for lack of proof. He claimed to know the location of hidden treasure, wrote pamphlets on alchemy, sold Egyptian amulets, and founded orphanages; he was a very 'modern' European.

But it is as promoter of Freemasonry that he is perhaps best remembered, and he was central to the acceptance of women into the Masonic community. Sadly for him it was Freemasonry that brought about his fall because in 1789 he was arrested in Rome for attempting to establish a lodge there. This led to his imprisonment in the Fortress of San Leo in Italy. While there is no clear evidence for seeing Freemasonry as a branch of the occult and the supernatural, it has been associated with the movement, which helps explain why the Italian authorities were so keen to supress it.

↑ The enigmatic and mysterious Count Cagliostro.

THE MAGNIFICENT SEVEN

FINDING A HOME FOR PERMANENT LONDONERS

London grew rapidly in the early Victorian period. In 1801 the population of the capital was just tipping the scales at a million souls, but by 1841 this had nearly doubled. With a rising populace came increased pressure on churchyard burials. It wasn't common practice to cremate the dead in nineteenth-century England and so the graveyards of the capital quickly began to fill up. Mortality was high, made worse by cholera epidemics (**see page 173**). The Church of England was reluctant to do anything about the problem, as their parishes made money from funerals.

There were some initiatives to tackle the problem of overcrowded plots; in 1832 George Camden set up the General Cemetery Company and Parliament granted them land at Kensal Green to establish a new burial ground. The success of Kensal Green and the passing of the Burial Act in 1852, which allowed the closure of existing graveyards to new internments, helped embed the idea that publicly funded cemeteries were a good idea.

Kensal Green was followed by West Norwood in south-east London in 1837, Highgate in 1839 (extended in 1854), Nunhead (south-east London), Brompton (west London), Abney Park, (Stoke Newington) in 1840, and Tower Hamlets in east London a year later. All were in part inspired by the example of Père Lachaise in Paris (ordered by Napoleon in 1804), and all serve as compelling visual reminders of the wealth of Victorian and Edwardian London and of the period's deep attachment to mourning the dead.

↑ The Magnificent Seven provided Londoners with an ordered system to bury and honour their dead.

HENRY SLADE
THE FRAUDULENT MEDIUM

Henry Slade, American spiritualist (c. 1836–1905), was a pioneer of 'spirit writing' (the mysterious appearance of messages from the spirit world). These would appear written in chalk on slates like those used in Victorian school rooms. His 'spirit guide' was his dead wife, Emily. He rose to fame in his native USA and in Europe, accruing a huge fortune.

Slade came to London in 1876, on his way to meet with Madame Blavatsky (**see page 86**) in Russia, demonstrating his skills as a medium and charging large amounts of money for private psychic consultations. However, two sceptics, Professor Ray Lankester and Dr Bryan Donkin, decided to catch him out. They successfully exposed Slade as a fraud, Lankester managing to grab the slate before the spirit of the deceased Mrs Slade could etch it, revealing the message already inscribed. Slade was charged with accepting money by false pretences and his prosecutors were able to call an expert witness, John Nevil Maskelyne (**see page 92**), a self-styled 'magician' performer and the scourge of fake mediums.

During the prosecution at Bow Street, Maskelyne demonstrated how Slade's consulting table was designed with a concealed mechanism allowing the user to write messages on a double-sided slate board while giving the impression that these were created by his 'spirit guide'. He was found guilty and given three months' hard labour. He was able to escape prison on a legal technicality and fled to France.

↑ Newspaper coverage of Slade's trial.

→ Highgate Cemetery in the 1840s, showing the Lebanon cedar and the catacombs.

SUICIDE BURIALS IN LONDON

A CURIOUS RITUAL TO DENY THE RESURRECTION

Until 1823, those who took their own lives were not buried on consecrated church land. Instead, suicides were interred, without rites, at the roadside, often with a stake driven through their heart. There was deep symbolism here: to kill oneself went against God's law and so the offender was refused the sacrament that even hanged criminals enjoyed. Burial at a crossroads or within the road was deliberate as it condemned the deceased to be forever disturbed, and not to 'rest in peace', as they would if they had been buried in a parish church yard. The stake ensured that on 'judgement day' they would be unable to rise again.

The law changed in 1823 and thereafter the bodies of suicides could be placed within the grounds of a church, albeit on the peripheries so that the sense of being forgotten was maintained. In the aftermath of the Ratcliffe Highway murders (**see page 42**) in December 1811 the body of the accused killer John Williams, who had committed suicide, was drawn to the junction of the Commercial Road and Cannon Street and buried in a shallow grave with a wooden stake in his torso.

Williams was probably the most high profile or notorious cadaver to be buried in this way, but his was not the last. In June 1823 a man named Griffiths who had committed patricide then killed himself, was interred at the end of Grosvenor Place in Knightsbridge.

MADAME BLAVATSKY

SPIRITUALIST AND FOUNDER OF THEOSOPHY

Madame Blavatsky was one of the most fascinating characters of the late nineteenth century. Born in 1831 in Yekaterinoslav (now in Ukraine, but in the 1830s in the Russian Empire), Helena Petrovna Blavatsky was one of a number of spiritualists operating across Europe in the late 1800s. In the 1880s, she co-founded the Theosophical Society in Madras, India.

Theosophy ('divine wisdom', from the Greek Theos, 'god' and Sophia, 'wisdom') was a belief that the many religions of the world had common themes and mythologies from which there was much to be learned. Followers of Theosophy believed in reincarnation, the existence of multiple spirit lives, and in karma. Perhaps the most incredible (in all senses of the word) thing about her was her claim to be able to send messages across the globe instantly by 'astral projection'. Blavatsky's claims to be in regular contact with 'a brotherhood of Great Masters' (the 'Mahatmas') came under intense scrutiny and she was accused of being a fraud. She travelled back to Europe, finally settling in London in 1887 where she remained until her death in May 1891.

While in the English capital, Blavatsky published her most important work, *The Secret Doctrine* (1888), which sets out the principles of Theosophy. Perhaps Blavatsky's greatest legacy was in opening Western hearts and minds to Eastern religion and spirituality, which was to become so influential in the twentieth century.

↑ Madame Blavatsky's legacy lasted long after her death in 1891.

THE COCK LANE GHOST

SCRATCHING FANNY, AND THE
EXPOSURE OF A DESPERATE FRAUD

Cock Lane is an unassuming alleyway close to the Old Bailey. In the Middle Ages it was synonymous with prostitution, which possibly explains its name (although it may equally refer to the trade in chickens at nearby Smithfield Market). In 1666 the Great Fire burned itself out at the top of the lane and a grateful City elite commissioned a statue of a golden boy (still present today) to mark its delivery from the flames. But it is for a long-forgotten and sensational ghost story that Cock Lane was once notorious.

In 1759 William Kent and his pregnant (but unmarried) lover Fanny Lynes moved into 20 Cock Lane. His landlord was Richard Parsons, a disreputable character in spite of his employment as a clerk at St Sepulchre's church. Constantly in debt and having borrowed money from his tenant without the ability to repay it, Parsons was keen to exploit any opportunity to avoid payment and enrich himself. He soon discovered that William and Fanny were unmarried and that her family held a grudge against Kent. Parsons decided he could use this to his advantage.

At some point in 1759, Fanny and Parsons' ten-year-old daughter Elizabeth (Betty) reported hearing scratching noises while William was away on a business trip. The pair had taken to sharing a bed, at first because Betty asked and latterly because Fanny enjoyed her company. The scratching was always in the bedroom where Betty slept. Rumours of a haunting grew in the neighbourhood. After an altercation over the debt, the Kents moved out, but the ghost tales continued. Then Fanny fell ill and died, most likely of smallpox. Richard Parsons saw his opportunity. He invited the Revd Moore, an Anglican with Methodist leanings, to visit Cock Lane to hear the noises for himself. Moore quickly became convinced that the house was haunted. Moreover, a rumour having been started by Parsons that Kent may have murdered Fanny, Moore decided that the noises he'd heard was her restless spirit returned to bring her lover to justice.

The house now became a focus for the curious, with Parsons charging anyone who dared to spend a couple of hours experiencing

the paranormal. William Kent, concerned both for his reputation and his life (if he was proven to be a killer) challenged the veracity of the Cock Lane ghost. In January 1762 it was finally revealed that the noises were being made by Betty on the instructions of her father. With the Cock Lane ghost story first a sensational news story and now a scandal, Parsons and his collaborators were tried before Lord Mansfield and convicted of fraud. Kent was compensated for the slur to his reputation and a terrified Richard Parsons was stood in the pillory (**see page 17**). Luckily for him the crowd treated him kindly, seeing him as pathetic character rather than a scheming villain. The story of 'scratching Fanny' was satirised by Oliver Goldsmith (author of *She Stoops to Conquer*) and the artist William Hogarth, while the established church made much of the gullibility of dissenting ministers like the Revd Moore who did fall for the scam.

↑ The Cock Lane ghost story as seen by a contemporary satirist (possibly Oliver Goldsmith), entitled *English Credulity or the Invisible Ghost*, 1762.

DEATH & THE SUPERNATURAL   89

PEPPER'S GHOST

A VICTORIAN TROMPE-L'ŒIL

On Christmas Eve 1862, visitors to the Royal Polytechnic Institution on Regent's Street were treated to a new phenomenon, the onstage appearance of a ghost! The spectral figure was Redlaw, the central character in Charles Dickens' *The Haunted Man and the Ghost's Bargain*. This story concerns a somewhat shy chemist who is troubled by his past. The novel's themes of memory, consciousness and illusion provided the perfect platform for John Henry Pepper, scientist, inventor and theatrical entertainer.

The Polytechnic was home to all sorts of strange and wonderful machines and devices, which would have cost you a shilling to view. For this, alongside the kaleidoscopes, cameras and other optical inventions, one could marvel at magic lantern shows on the main stage. And it was here that Pepper used Dickens' novel (and the accompanying illustrations by John Tenniel), to demonstrate a new invention, which was to become the eponymous 'Pepper's Ghost'. The act required the use of a piece of glass, hidden from the audience, and a light which allowed the projection of an actor to appear onstage seemingly among other, more corporeal, characters.

The effect was astonishing, but although Pepper pioneered it, he did not invent it. Henry Dircks was its true creator but despite Pepper being keen to give him credit (and equal rights to any money generated by it), Dircks' name has largely been forgotten. Meanwhile, every time Pepper exhibited his 'ghost' the curious, including the scientist Michael Faraday, tried, but failed, to work out how it was done.

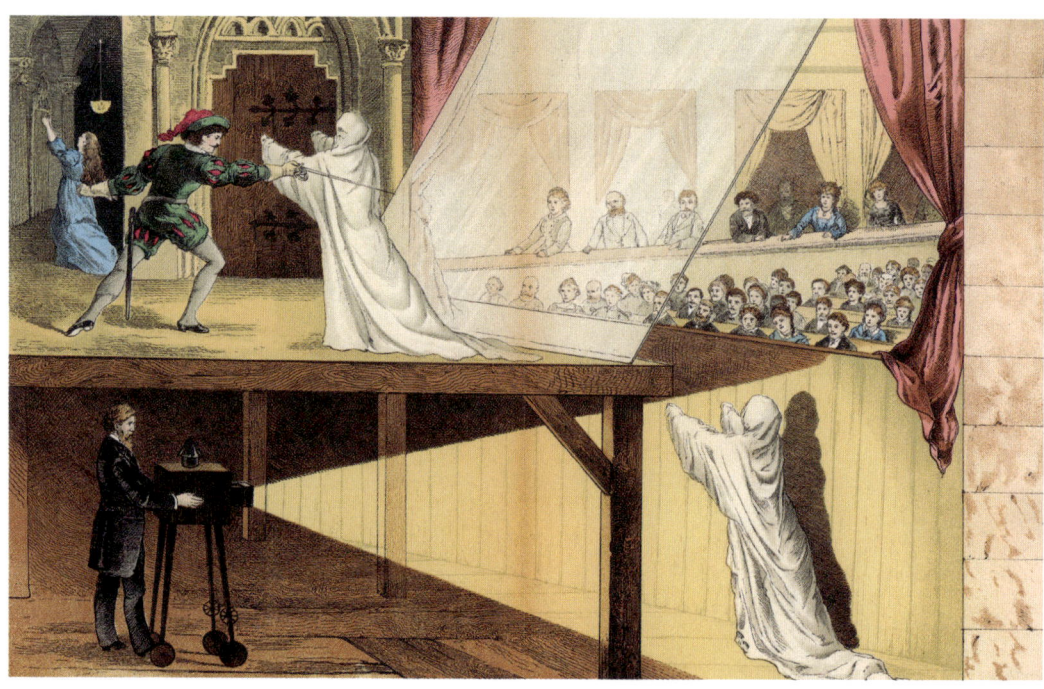

THE GHOST OF ALEXANDER POPE
A POET WHO SIMPLY WISHED TO BE LEFT IN PEACE

In 1830 the grave of the poet Alexander Pope was opened and his skull removed. The poet's skull allegedly ended up in the collection of Johann Spurzheim, a German physician who specialised in phrenology, the pseudoscientific study of the shape of skulls to understand the workings of the mind.

Whether Spurzheim obtained Alexander Pope's skull or not, the fact that his last resting place by the Thames was desecrated seems to have precipitated his spectral being to manifest itself. From 1830 Pope's ghost was occasionally seen at St Mary's Church in Twickenham 'perambulating the churchyard and the aisles, muttering and sometimes raving at the top of his voice'. The ghostly figure would then fade away 'accompanied', it is said 'by a dreadful paroxysm of coughing'.

Pope had died in 1744 and is remembered as one of the most talented writers of the Enlightenment. He died of dropsy (now identified as oedema) and acute asthma after a lifetime of suffering with a form of tuberculosis, which perhaps explains the coughing that is associated with his restless spirit. Pope might have enjoyed the idea that his ghost would haunt future generations; in 1717 he wrote a satirical poem entitled *Sandy's Ghost* of which the following lines form a part:

> Hear how a Ghost in dead of Night,
> With saucer Eyes of Fire,
> In woeful wise did sore affright
> A Wit and courtly 'Squire.

↑ A contemporary engraving of Alexander Pope.

←← A fabulous depiction of Pepper's Ghost deployed as a stage special effect.

Perhaps in death Pope was indeed able to unnerve the wealthy squires of leafy Twickenham.

THE EGYPTIAN HALL

ENGLAND'S HOME OF MYSTERY

In 1812, in what has been dubbed the first wave of 'Egyptomania', a new exhibition space opened on Piccadilly, opposite what is now the Burlington Arcade. Its purpose was to house William Bullock's extensive collection of curiosities, which he charged visitors a shilling to view. If you stepped inside you could see a huge range of weaponry, antiquities from Greece and Rome, plus stuffed animals from all over the world. The 'London Museum' (as it was called) even housed Napoleon's carriage, captured after Waterloo.

The hall was sold in 1825 and its new owners staged temporary exhibitions and performances featuring magicians and 'freak shows'. Among the acts to appear at the Egyptian Hall were Henri Robin, a French magician who performed illusions and tricks to delight his audience, one of which involved the spirit of a drummer boy who had died in 1854 at the Battle of Inkerman in the Crimean War.

John Nevil Maskelyne was another prominent magician whose aptitude with engineering and machinery (he had trained as a watchmaker) made him a popular performer. He also abhorred false mediums and intervened to expose those who profited from the public's gullibility (**see page 83**). With his partner, George Alfred Cooke, Maskelyne created the 'Box Escape' trick where he miraculously found his way out of a cabinet encircled with chains. The pair also performed one of the first levitation tricks. Sadly, the hall is now gone, demolished in 1905 for more shops.

↓ The magnificent Egyptian Hall on Piccadilly, which attracted thousands to see its many 'curiosities' and performances by magicians.

PHANTASMAGORIA
A MAGIC LANTERN SHOW FOR HALLOWE'EN

Early nineteenth-century audiences at the Lyceum Theatre in London flocked to see one of the great phenomena of the age, the phantasmagoria. Pioneered by magicians and entertainers like Paul Philidor or Étienne-Gaspard Robertson, the phantasmagoria used optical illusions to bring supernatural horror stories to the stage.

The effect was created using magic lanterns; devices that used a light source (typically candles) and a series of optical lenses to project images onto a surface or screen. Magic lantern shows are perhaps best described as early examples of 3D projection or cinema, which held a genuine fascination for nineteenth-century theatregoers. The focus of phantasmagoria was on horror and the supernatural, while more conventional magic lantern shows could represent anything from light entertainment to the natural world.

Fascination with the dead and, increasingly through the 1800s, with the spirit world, allowed the unscrupulous to experiment with ways of deceiving the gullible. So, phantasmagoria was also a way of demonstrating how it was possible to project the images of ghosts, devils and other supernatural beings via scientific means, thereby exposing the charlatans who claimed to be able to invoke the spirit world or commune with the dead.

↓ A phantasmagoria projects a ghostly figure to the shock and delight of a nineteenth-century audience.

50 BERKELEY SQUARE

THE MOST HAUNTED TOWN HOUSE IN LONDON?

From the 1870s 50 Berkeley Square, in London's fashionable Mayfair, seems to have garnered a reputation for hauntings. Several stories, including entries in the well-known Victorian publication *Notes & Queries*, detail reports of supernatural occurrences, although none have ever been substantiated. It was suggested that at some point a young woman had jilted her fiancé at the property, sending him into a madness that caused his spirit to haunt the place.

One account describes a housemaid who was driven mad by something she saw in one room, and was found convulsed on the floor, and who later died in St George's Hospital. Another tells of a visitor, sceptical of the rumours of supernatural activity, who insisted, much against the advice of the household, that he be allowed to sleep in that same room overnight. The next morning he was discovered in exactly the same position that the maid had been, writhing on the floor.

The only consistent fact about 50 Berkeley Square, for much of the late 1800s, is that it was uninhabited (by the living at least). Empty properties are often the subject of ghostly rumours, especially those – like number 50 – which were seemingly impossible to rent out or sell. Whether this was because the place was haunted, or because its uninhabited status made it easier to associate with the supernatural, or simply that the landlord was demanding too high a fee, will have to remain a mystery.

GHOSTS AT THE TOWER OF LONDON

THE CAPITAL'S MOST HAUNTED SPACE

Given that the Tower has dominated the capital for over a thousand years it is hardly surprising to find that several ghosts are supposed to haunt its ramparts, towers and chambers. In 1814 the Keeper of the Crown Jewels and his wife were scared by seeing 'a cylindrical figure, like a glass tube about four inches in diameter hovering between the ceiling and their dining table'. The tube's content appeared to be a fluid, 'white and blue in colour, constantly rolling within the container' and when the Keeper tried to attack the apparition, it vanished into thin air.

No one could provide a natural explanation for the incident and so a supernatural one was transposed: in the days leading up to her death on the block, Anne Boleyn had been imprisoned in a room on that site. Other ghostly sightings at the Tower are associated with those who, like Henry VIII's ill-fated queen, met their end there. Sir Walter Raleigh's ghost is said to haunt the place, as do those of Guy Fawkes and Lady Jane Grey (the nine-day queen).

The Queen's House is reputed to be visited by the ghost of Lady Arbella Stuart, who was imprisoned by James I, and who died of starvation within its walls. In total there are reputed to be thirteen ghosts at the fortress, which, given the huge numbers of people imprisoned, tortured and executed there, seems quite a low level of disgruntled supernatural manifestation.

→ A prisoner in the Tower is visited by a woman's ghost, could it be Anne Boleyn or Lady Jane Grey?

FORTUNE TELLING
EXPLOITING THE DESPERATE AND GULLIBLE

For as long as mankind has existed, we've been keen to know what 'fate' has in store for us. In the medieval and early modern periods 'wise women' (or witches as contemporaries often saw them) would offer advice in exchange for money or goods. Fortune tellers were a regular feature of country and horse fairs, and travelling communities would usually include those who could read palms, cards, or tea leaves. Witchcraft was a capital offence until 1736 when a new offence of claiming magical powers was created. Thereafter those suspected of defrauding the gullible with promises of future happiness could be, and were, prosecuted before magistrates and juries.

In 1834, Ellen Morgan was transported to Australia for the theft of a half crown and 8 shillings. Morgan had conned her victim out of that sum on the pretext of telling her fortune. In 1880, 'Methveston, the Great Seer, Philosopher and Astrologer' (aka John Major) appeared at Southwark Police Court charged with fraudulently 'obtaining sums of money from various persons [...] by pretending to tell their fortunes'. Having heard that Major was a serial offender who had duped hundreds of people, the magistrate sent him to face the music at the Surrey Assizes.

Old Bailey records show several similar cases, proving perhaps that there will always be those who are willing to pay for an insight into the future, however unlikely or irrational the claims of those purporting to offer this service might be.

← Fortune telling in the early nineteenth century; young women were especially vulnerable to predictions of love and a 'happy marriage'.

DEATH & THE SUPERNATURAL   97

↑ Two young boys learn about their future from Indian birds supposedly gifted with powers of divination.

← A fortune teller reveals the future in tea leaves.

SPRING-HEELED JACK
THE TERROR OF LONDON

On 6 March 1838, Lucy Scales was walking home with her sister along Green Dragon Alley in Limehouse. Up ahead Lucy noticed someone approaching them who appeared to be dressed in a cloak and hood, lurking in the shadows. To her horror he came towards the sisters and 'spurted a large quantity of blue flame' into her face. Lucy fainted, her sister screamed, and the demonic figure ran away.

The attack on the Scales sisters was not the first strange encounter that year; just two weeks earlier, on 20 February, Jane Alsop had been attacked outside her home in a village outside Bow, also in east London. On this occasion she'd been summoned by someone she thought was a policeman, who claimed to have apprehended 'Spring-Heeled Jack'. It was a sham and when Jane was close enough the man launched a vicious assault, ripping her clothes and skin with his claws and tearing out clumps of her hair. Rescued by her sister, Jane was later able to describe her assailant. She told police that he wore 'a very large helmet' and a tight-fitting costume which 'appeared to resemble white oil-skin'.

Over the next few weeks there were more sightings of the strange character who was dubbed 'Spring-Heeled Jack'. It was claimed he could leap ten-foot walls, breathe fire, that his eyes glowed like red coals, and that he wore a suit of flexible armour. It is likely that 'Jack' inspired copycat attackers, and plenty of false sightings, as panic about him spread. There were reports of attacks in other parts of London and Surrey, and as far away as the Kent coast and Cornwall. There were also unfounded rumours that the attacks were part of an elaborate upper-class dare, perpetrated by decadent members of aristocracy like the 'Mad' Marquis of Waterford.

By the end of April 1838 'Jack' had dropped out of the news, but this was not the end of the story. In 1863 a new 'Penny Dreadful' story was published entitled *Spring-Heeled Jack: The Terror of London*. There were forty issues, each eight pages long and illustrated. This 'Jack' had become some sort of vigilante, sometimes helping save others from evil rather than being a prankster villain himself. The series firmly rooted him in Victorian popular culture until in 1877 the 'actual' Spring-Heeled Jack made his comeback. 'Jack' was first sighted at Aldershot Barracks, and then leaping over the Newport Arch in Lincoln, before again disappearing once more from the news.

There remains considerable doubt, both to the identity of 'Jack', and the extent of his (or their) attacks and abilities. He very quickly became something of an urban legend, and separating the truth from myth and fictional representations of Spring-Heeled Jack is all but impossible. In many ways he was a creation of Victorian urban popular culture, which blended the folk stories and traditions of the many communities that made up nineteenth-century London, with the fears of the 'modern'. Much of this mythologising would later be ascribed to another 'Jack', Jack the Ripper (**see page 30**).

→ Spring-Heeled Jack from an early twentieth century penny dreadful.

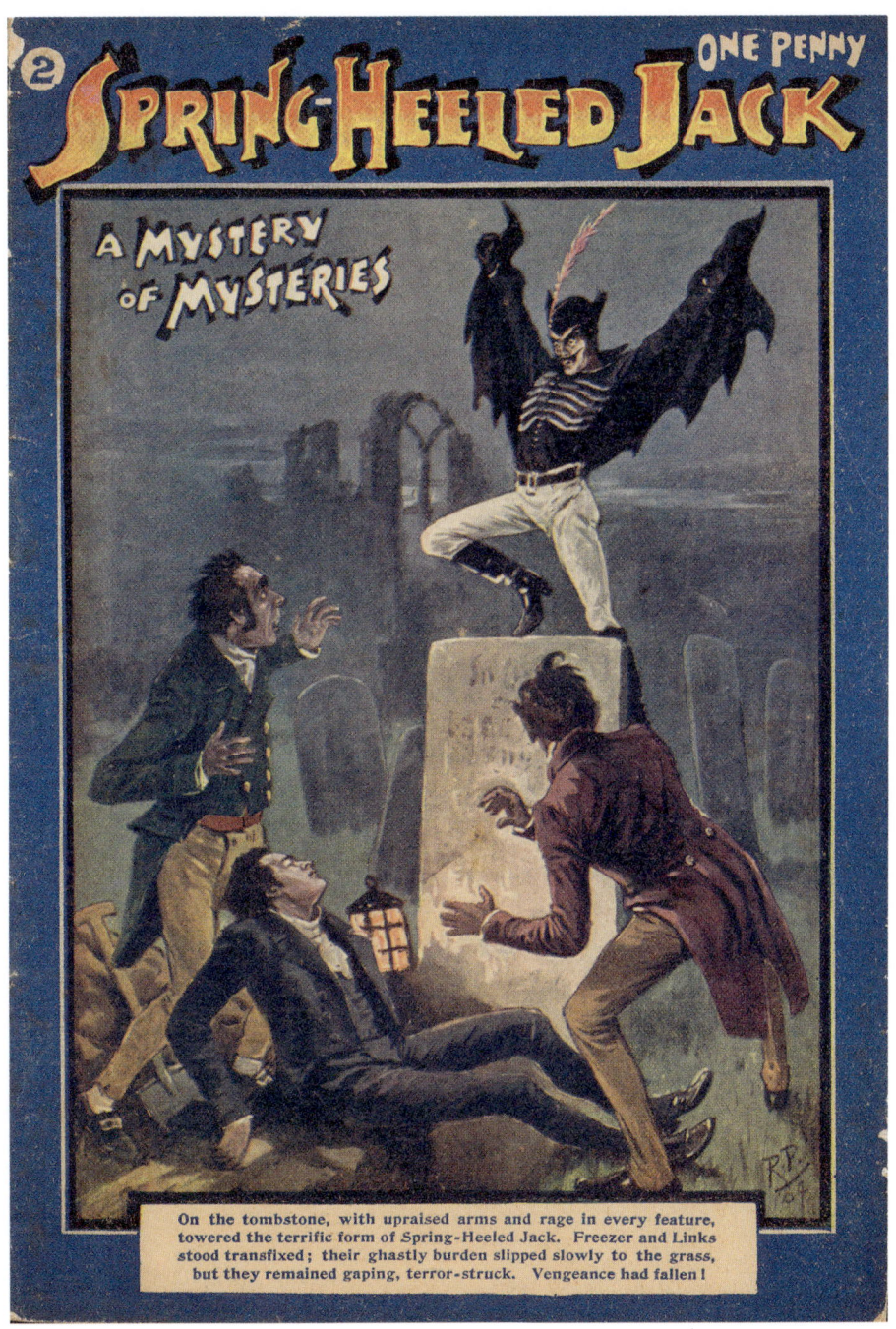

THE HYDE PARK PET CEMETERY

A RESTING PLACE FOR THE WEALTHY'S FAITHFUL FRIENDS

Within the grounds of Hyde Park is a cemetery that few will have visited. In the 1800s Victoria Lodge was occupied by a Mr Winbridge who for many years had been servant to the Duke of Cambridge, cousin to Queen Victoria. The duke was the titular Ranger at Hyde Park and he appointed Winbridge as his gatekeeper.

At some point in 1881 a well-heeled member of the public asked if he could bury his pet dog in the gatekeeper's garden. Winbridge kindly granted the request. Similar applications followed, and thereafter it became *the* place for society Victorians to inter their canine (and occasionally feline) companions after death. Some 300 or more animals were buried in the small cemetery before it finally closed in 1903 having exceeded its capacity.

Among the extant memorials are several that suggest interesting stories, none more so than that of Balu, a dog whose death was attributed to poisoning by 'the cruel Swiss', or Topper, a police dog who constantly ran away from his handlers, preferring to spend his time with the wealthy Victorians who promenaded in the park. Today the pet cemetery can be visited as part of official tours of Hyde Park, but it is no longer open for internments.

↓ A Victorian family remembers their much-loved pet.

THE PRIMROSE HILL NECROPOLIS

THE PYRAMID OF DEATH THAT NEVER WAS

While many of the sites described in this volume have changed their use or no longer exist, here is one that never existed at all. What is fascinating, however, is that its construction was mooted at all. In the 1820s, London was struggling with the problem of where to bury the dead (**see page 82**).

One idea, put forward by Thomas Wilson in 1820, was the building of a huge mausoleum at Primrose Hill or Shooters Hill. Wilson's design featured a number of options, all embracing the nineteenth-century obsession with Egyptology (**see page 92**). The most extravagant of these was a giant pyramid, its base a large as Russell Square and its apex taller than St Paul's Cathedral. Its multiple alcoves would have had space for 5,167,104 coffins, so had Wilson's plan seen the light of day it might not yet be full.

It would have cost as much as £7 million (close to £600 million at today's prices) to build, but much of that would have been quickly recouped, Wilson believed, in the fees charged for funerary arrangements. The necropolis would have dominated the London skyline rather as the Shard and other office buildings do today, as a daily reminder to our ancestors of their mortality. Perhaps it is understandable that objections ensured it was never built.

↓ A bucolic vision of Primrose Hill (without the necropolis that might have topped it).

THE HUMMUMS

A COVENT GARDEN MYSTERY

Imagine, if you can, Covent Garden market in the 1700s, as a bustling centre of trade in all things, including sex. Where now the visitor will find expensive eateries, fashionable boutiques and street entertainers, Covent Garden was, until the late twentieth century, a less salubrious destination. Many of the capital's brothels were in and around Covent Garden, and in nearby Seven Dials poverty and criminality were facts of life. Located at the south-east corner of Covent Garden's Little Piazza, was the Hummums.

'Hummums' is possibly a corruption of the Turkish word 'hamam' for bath, suggesting this was the original purpose of the building. By the eighteenth century the Hummums was notorious as a bagnio (brothel) and was frequented by London's most decadent residents. The Hummums is probably the setting for William Hogarth's *A Midnight Modern Conversation* (1732) which features as a central character Parson Ford, seemingly unaffected by the drunken chaos around him. Ford died the year before the etching was published and is referred to from the painting by Boswell in his *Life of Samuel Johnson*.

The Hummums was later turned into a respectable hotel and Dr Johnson recounts how a waiter there apparently met with Parson Ford as he made his way to the cellar, only to have it explained to him by his colleagues that the man had died several years previously. At this the poor man fell ill and, having recovered enough to go out, muttering darkly about delivering a message to a lady at Ford's behest, was never seen again.

→ William Hogarth's satirical engraving, *A Midnight Modern Conversation*, 1732.

DRURY LANE
THE MOST HAUNTED THEATRE IN LONDON

The Theatre Royal on Drury Lane has existed in some incarnation since 1663, the oldest theatre site in continuous use in the capital. It survived the Great Fire but went up in flames in 1674, prompting the first of three rebuilds. Given its age and the number of artists that have trodden the boards there it is not surprising to discover that the theatre is haunted.

The most well-established ghost is unnamed, simply known as 'the man in grey'. This apparition in eighteenth-century costume is said to be the spirit of a murdered man whose skeleton was found during renovations to the theatre in 1848. His appearance is taken as a good luck sign by theatre folk. Less positive seems to be the ghost of Charles Macklin, an actor from the early 1700s who accidently killed a colleague in a fight.

Moving into the Victorian period the ghost of Dan Leno, or rather his scent (he was known to perfume himself with lavender water) has been known to play tricks on the unwary. Joseph Grimaldi, who gave some of his most famous comic performances as a clown at Drury Lane is also said to appear in spectral form. Grimaldi's ghost is supposedly more benign, offering actors advice and encouragement rather than causing them to trip over or fall off stage as Leno's is alleged to do. The Theatre Royal is very old and very old buildings are frequently associated with the supernatural, so keep an eye out if you go to visit.

← Joseph Grimaldi, a pioneer of clowning and celebrated as 'the funniest man in the world' in his day. His ghost is said to be one of several that haunt the theatre.

SOUTH LONDON GHOST SIGHTINGS
PHANTOMS IN PECKHAM AND THE CAMBERWELL GHOST

As London's suburbs developed and the capital spread out, to the north and south, the urban sprawl gradually began to swallow previously rural areas which retained some pockets of countryside, along with long-held folk beliefs and traditions. Perhaps this contributed to the persistence of false rumours and supposed sightings of mysterious spectral figures like Spring-Heeled Jack (**see page 100**).

There were the appearances of two ghosts in Peckham, some years apart, one of which allegedly threw stones at houses and at people, and another which simply scared locals witless by leaping out at them. Then, in December 1872, as two teenage girls were on their way to church with their governess, the younger one thought she saw something move in the shadows. She watched, horrified, as a ghostly figure approached her with its arms extended ahead of it, zombie-like, dressed from head to toe in white. The young woman screamed and ran back to her sister and governess, thoroughly frightened by the encounter.

A search of the area was instigated on the following morning, but this revealed nothing except that the place where the 'Camberwell Ghost' had been seen was an ideal spot for anyone wishing to hide and play a practical joke on the unwary. The 'ghost' could have hidden behind a wall and archway with the perfect view of any approaching pedestrians. This, then, is the most likely explanation for the so-called 'Camberwell Ghost' and many other supernatural manifestations that were reported in the pages of the Victorian newspapers.

← The 'Camberwell Ghost' terrifies a passing pony and trap driver.

DENS OF VICE
& INIQUITY

THE LONDON BURKERS

RESURRECTION MEN WHO PREYED ON THE VULNERABLE

Throughout the eighteenth century anatomy schools had been able to obtain a relatively plentiful supply of dead bodies to use to train new surgeons. This was because the 1752 Murder Act had decreed that the bodies of executed murderers would be donated to them to dissect. This supply had all but dried up by the 1820s, when the number of available corpses dwindled to around fifty-five annually, while the medical schools needed ten times that number. This presented opportunities for 'resurrection men' who raided graves and sold cadavers to the hospitals. Recently disinterred bodies could fetch a good price and bodies were unearthed from burial grounds across London.

As graverobbing was so widespread, families protected graves with grills and fences, and watch houses were built close to graveyards to catch graverobbers in the act. There were watch houses at Hampstead and Walthamstow, and one still survives in Spitalfields. In Edinburgh in 1828, William Burke and William Hare, two Irish migrants to Scotland, took bodysnatching one step further, by murdering victims and selling the corpses to the surgeon Robert Knox. In the wake of the Burke and Hare scandal, medical schools and hospitals and resurrection men became targets for angry crowds, fuelled by rumours of children being killed and sold for anatomising. Stories of 'burking' created a moral panic dubbed 'Burkiphobia' or the 'Burking Mania'.

John Bishop and Thomas Williams were London's most infamous resurrection men. As part of the 'Bethnal Green Gang' they had supplied somewhere between 500 and 1,000 bodies to anatomy schools across London.

In July 1830, Bishop rented a property at Nova Scotia Gardens, a desperately rough and impoverished area in the East End, and he and his fellow gang members switched from graverobbing to outright murder. In November 1831 they tried to sell the corpse of a fourteen-year-old boy, but the freshness of the body and the lack of burial information raised suspicions and they were arrested. A search of 3 Nova Scotia Gardens suggested foul play and Bishop, Williams and James May were convicted of murder at the Old Bailey and sentenced to death.

As they waited to hang in Newgate Prison, Bishop and Williams confessed to drugging their fourteen-year-old victim with a rum and laudanum mix before drowning him upside down in a barrel of water. Other victims included a homeless woman they'd found on the street in Shoreditch and another boy whose body they sold for eight guineas. Their confession saved James May, whose sentence was commuted to transportation to Van Dieman's Land. Bishop and Williams were hanged outside Newgate Prison and their bodies given over to the surgeons to be dissected.

The Nova Scotia slum was eventually demolished and today Columbia Street flower market covers the ground on which it once stood. In 1832, Parliament passed the Anatomy Act which decreed that any pauper who died in the workhouse without family could be disposed of however the authorities saw fit. This often meant the bodies were sold to teaching hospitals like St Bart's to be dissected.

→ Two police officers on graveyard patrol.

DENS OF VICE & INIQUITY   III

SUSANNAH HILL
I'VE HANGED A MAN, AND HANGED HIM TOO LONG!

Susannah Hill was one of many young women who arrived in London in the 1700s hoping to find their fortune. She was looking for her lover who had abandoned her, pregnant in Somerset, and reneged on his promise to fetch her to the metropolis once he was established. By 1791 Susannah was working as a prostitute in Vine Street and on 2 September she entertained a customer with a very unusual request. Francis Kotzwara (Kočvara) was an Austrian musician and composer of some note, resident in London, who performed at the King's Theatre (now Her Majesty's, at the Haymarket).

At first Kotzwara asked Susannah to take a knife to his penis, which she refused. She did help him attach a rope to a door handle so that he might enhance his sexual pleasure through self-strangulation. Auto-erotic asphyxiation was not unknown in the 1790s: the Marquis de Sade described the practice in *Justine*. Unfortunately, it all went wrong for Kotzwara and Susannah because she left him hanging too long and he choked to death. She ran out of the house shouting: 'I've hanged a man, and I am afraid he is dead!' She was promptly arrested and charged with murder.

The case at the Old Bailey collapsed and was not reported, as the authorities had imposed a ban on repeating scandalous sexual content in the Old Bailey Proceedings. Indeed, we might not have known about this case had not a prurient pamphleteer decided to write up the story for public information and entertainment.

↑ The cover picture of *Modern Propensities; Or, an Essay on the Art of Strangling*, published anonymously in 1791. It shows Susannah tying the composer to a door handle.

HOLYWELL STREET
A FOUNTAIN OF IMPURITY

↑ Readers browse the bookshops on Holywell Street.

Until it was destroyed at the turn of the twentieth century to make way for The Aldwych and Kingsway, Holywell Street near the Strand was synonymous with pornography and vice. The meandering thoroughfare which linked east and west London and the City had been a thriving retail area which had begun to decline in the 1700s. By the mid-eighteenth century it was a centre for the second-hand clothes trade, with many Jewish businesses. In the nineteenth century it was dubbed 'the London ghetto'.

Holywell Street (so-called because tradition held that it once had a well which revived pilgrims bound for Canterbury) had, by the 1840s, been populated by numerous booksellers, many of whom were selling what disapproving commentators descried as 'low publications'. This was Victorian euphemism for obscene prints and illustrated texts, photographs and other printed material which offended public morality in an age that placed considerable store by 'respectability'.

Holywell Street's labyrinthian layout, combined with its poor reputation, ensured that it represented everything that was wrong with the capital for some observers. It was seen as a polluted space, both physically and morally, and there were multiple plans drawn up to redevelop it. Against this were voices who argued that Holywell Street, with its Tudor buildings and age-old reminders of its better days, was one of the last remaining vestiges of an 'old London' that was fast disappearing. The work of redevelopment finally began in 1900 and The Aldwych opened in 1905.

DENS OF VICE & INIQUITY   113

THE MAIDEN TRIBUTE OF MODERN BABYLON

A GIRL OF THIRTEEN BOUGHT FOR £5!

In 1885 William T. Stead, an influential newspaper editor, waded into a debate that had been exercising Parliament. The Criminal Law Amendment bill proposed raising the age of consent for girls from thirteen to sixteen. Change was needed, supporters argued, to protect girls from being trafficked to the Continent to work as prostitutes. Stead had transformed the *Pall Mall Gazette* into a successful weekly, and recognised an opportunity to promote his belief that the media had a key role to play in changing society.

Stead discovered a trade in teenage virgins. To expose this, he tasked Rebecca Jarrett, a former procuress (a woman who found women for brothels) with acquiring a thirteen-year-old to prove it was easily done. Jarrett found a woman willing to allow her daughter, Eliza Armstrong, to be taken into service for £5 (£550 today). What happened next is unclear but it is likely that Eliza was prepared for a transactional sexual encounter. Jarrett may have used chloroform to induce sleep, then undressed Eliza and left her for a client. The 'client' was Stead and there's no suggestion that he carried his pretence to its conclusion.

Thereafter Eliza was whisked off to Paris and lodged with the Salvation Army. Meanwhile Stead wrote up his story issuing a warning to 'all those who are squeamish […] prudish, selfishly oblivious to the horrible realities which torment those whose lives are passed in the London inferno'. The exposé ('The Maiden Tribute of Modern Babylon'), drew on the Greek myth of the minotaur and the annual sacrifice of young people. It was sensational journalism and sold out in hours. In the aftermath, serious questions were asked about Stead's methods, partly as a result of jealousy from his rivals and because Mrs Armstrong found herself subject to criticism for selling her daughter. Stead and Jarrett were tried for kidnapping. Stead defended himself, and he and Jarrett were convicted (on the technicality that Eliza's father had not given his permission for her to enter service), with Stead going to Holloway for three months and Jarrett for six.

Stead's campaign helped change the law: the Criminal Law Amendment Act raised the age of consent, and anyone procuring girls under thirteen for prostitution overseas were made liable to a life sentence. Stead's actions raised awareness of the 'virgin trade' and helped increase protection for young working-class girls. In 1912, Stead was one of many who drowned when the *Titanic* sank.

↑ William T. Stead is credited with pioneering investigative journalism in the 1880s.

WIFE SELLING
AN OUTRAGE UPON DECENCY?

In 1815 a wealthy cattle grazier brought his beautiful young wife to Smithfield Market and sold her to a horse trader for the sum of fifty guineas (about £4,000 today) and the purchaser's horse. The young woman sported a silk halter, a material indicative of her social class, but also a reminder that she was the possession of her husband, who was free to dispose of his property as he saw fit to the highest bidder.

While this incident might shock a modern reader, wife sales were, if not commonplace, certainly not unknown in the eighteenth and nineteenth centuries. They were part of customary practice and took place across England, invariably at markets like Smithfield and other public spaces. Men brought their wives, some form of halter was worn, an auctioneer conducted the sale, money was exchanged, usually followed by a shared drink, and the woman left with her new husband. Almost always 'sales' had been agreed beforehand; the notion that women were sold like cattle at auction was a falsehood propagated by those offended by it.

This was a plebeian tradition, so the sale of a middling man's wife was unusual (and probably made the newspapers). Divorce was not allowed under ecclesiastical or civil law in the period and so 'wife selling' allowed couples to separate and legally re-marry. Holding these rituals in public was probably more to do with confirming that one relationship had ended and another begun, than a demonstration of overbearing patriarchy.

↓ A wife is 'sold'. The man nearest to her seems to be examining her as one might a horse, suggesting this image was drawn to critique the practice.

DENS OF VICE & INIQUITY   115

THE CLEVELAND STREET SCANDAL

A CRIMINAL CONSPIRACY OF THE GUARDIANS OF PUBLIC MORALITY AND LAW!

If the 'Maiden Tribute' had exposed the exploitation of young girls (**see page 114**), the Cleveland Street scandal, while largely covered up to protect the guilty, reminded people that boys were also vulnerable. That a male brothel operated from 19 Cleveland Street was unknown to most people until news broke in January 1890. The premises had been raided in September 1889, and a number of high-profile individuals were interrogated at the Marylebone Police Court. The affair was initiated because a Post Office telegraph boy, found in possession of more money than he should have, explained that he was being paid for 'certain activities' in Cleveland Street.

The British press was reluctant to report the case because many of those implicated were wealthy aristocrats, possibly including an heir to the throne. It therefore fell to the American and colonial press to carry the story, with a New Zealand paper stating: 'A list of offenders features future Dukes, the sons of Dukes, Peers, Hebrew financiers, many honourable persons, and several officers of the Imperial Army'.

When the *North London Press* did print names, its editor was arrested for libel. The only other prosecution was that of Henry Newlove, a Post Office clerk, and George Veck, who had been sacked from the Telegraph Office for 'improper conduct' with boys. Both men pleaded guilty to indecency and were sent to prison.

→ The scandal gave the newspapers plenty of rich imagery even if the real culprits' names were concealed.

THE BARTHOLOMEW FAIR
A RITUAL OF VICE AND LAWLESSNESS

Until the 1760s when the authorities largely managed to suppress them, Londoners could enjoy several days of entertainment at one of a number of street fairs. These had begun life in the medieval period and had survived despite a growing demand for order in the Georgian city. There were various May Day fairs, and local fairs at Tottenham Court, Greenwich and the Horn Fair at Charlton. Southwark Fair was held in September and was notably anarchic, but the most important and biggest London festival was Bartholomew Fair which could trace its history back to the twelfth century.

Revellers at Bartholomew could expect to see all manner of street theatre, including puppet shows, performing animals, jugglers and musicians. They might sample a selection of street food and drink was plentiful (something that the authorities made much of in their condemnation). Just as concerning to the City's leaders was the gambling, prostitution and thefts which accompanied the festivities. In 1735 the City managed to limit the Fair to a few days of the week, but public pressure meant that they were unable to ban it as they had done with Southwark (in 1763) or May Day a year later.

In the end it was the Victorians that succeeded in closing down Bartholomew Fair in 1855, as part of wider move to 'improve' London. The fair took place close to Smithfield Market which was repurposed from a livestock to a 'dead meat' market between 1852 and 1855, as a result of the same improvement movement.

← Engraved illustration of the Bartholomew Fair, 1721.

JOSEPH MERRICK
THE ELEPHANT MAN

There was a tradition, well-established by the late 1880s, of exhibiting 'curiosities' for public entertainment. In 1837, among celebrations for the new Queen, Victoria, visitors to the Hyde Park Fair could stare at a dwarf, a 'Living Skeleton', a two-headed lady, and other marvels of nature. Meanwhile so-called 'Penny Exhibitions' proliferated, their name reflecting the entrance fee, and it was at one of these on Whitechapel High Street that Joseph Carey Merrick came to prominence in 1886.

Merrick had been born in Leicester in 1862 and from the age of five developed a physical disorder which dramatically altered his appearance and affected his growth. It is possible that Merrick suffered with Proteus syndrome, which causes overgrowth in bones, muscles, fatty tissues and lymphatic vessels. Merrick's life-story is clouded by competing histories but it seems possible that he was kept in a workhouse until he escaped in 1883 to make a living by 'performing' in a 'freak show'.

While being exhibited in an East End 'penny gaff', Merrick was seen by Dr Frederick Treves who worked at the London Hospital opposite. Treves had Merrick admitted in 1886 and soon recognised that his physical condition was deteriorating quickly. Merrick became well known in Victorian society, receiving visitors in his rooms at the London Hospital, and even travelling for holidays. He died in his sleep in April 1890 at the age of twenty-seven, the cause of death recorded as asphyxia attributed to a broken neck. His skeleton is retained within the collection of the Royal London's pathology department.

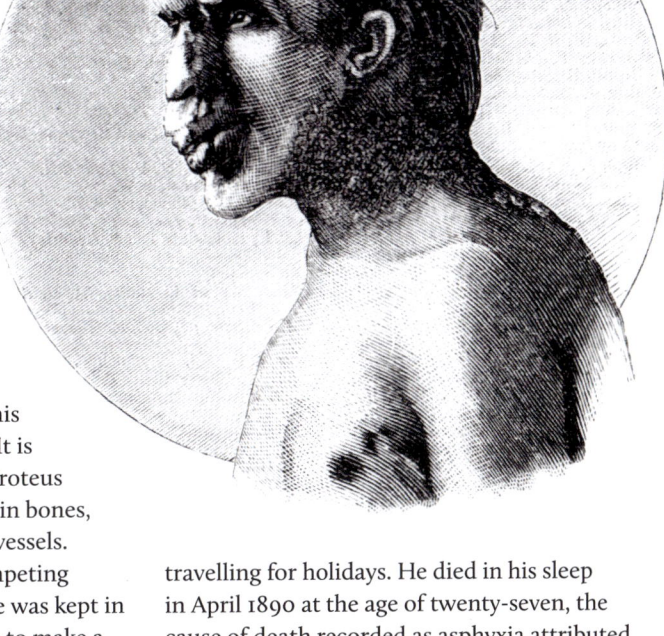

↑ Joseph Merrick, whose medical condition earned him the sobriquet 'The Elephant Man' when he was exhibited at an East End 'penny gaff'.

DENS OF VICE & INIQUITY

LONDON'S PLEASURE GARDENS

ENTERTAINMENTS TO SUIT ALL TASTES AND MORALS

Eighteenth-century Londoners could enjoy a variety of 'pleasures' at a number of gardens, spas and pleasure grounds, established from the reign of Queen Anne. Sadler's Wells, Islington Spa and Bagnigge Wells offered visitors 'medicinal waters' to rival the more well-known spas at Bath and Tunbridge Wells.

The four most important pleasure gardens in the capital were Cuper's, near Somerset House, Marylebone Gardens, Ranelagh Gardens in Chelsea, and Vauxhall Pleasure Gardens. These offered entertainments as well as a space to promenade and be seen. Ranelagh's Rotunda was its biggest attraction and it charged half a crown (2s 6d) for entry. The others cost a shilling, or you could buy season tickets. Entertainments included music, dancing, acrobats, masquerades, firework displays, food and tea; all standard pastimes of middling and elite society.

However, while these locations traded on the gentile nature of their clientele, and the civilised and respectable entertainments they provided them, there was a less salubrious side to places like Ranelagh and Vauxhall. Gambling, cock fights and bare-knuckle boxing took place, while gatherings of the wealthy inevitably attracted criminals, as a result of which gardens employed watchmen. It was also hard to prevent sex workers using the venues as a place to pick up clients, while plenty of men attended the gardens precisely because of the opportunities for sexual encounters. Drunkenness, 'boorish' behaviour and rape were also common. These were not safe spaces for everyone, and existed almost outside societal rules. It is unsurprising then that they did not last long in a more conservative Victorian world.

← Ladies and gentlemen enjoy an afternoon at Vauxhall Pleasure Gardens.

→ Ranelagh Gardens' famous rotunda.

VIEWS IN VAUXHALL GARDENS.

1. Fountain at Back of Orchestra. 2. Ruins at End of Walk. 3. The Orchestra. 4. Neptune's Fountain
5. Old Entrance to Vauxhall Gardens. 6. Back of Orchestra.

GAMBLING IN THE CAPITAL

GAMES OF CHANCE FOR ALL LEVELS OF SOCIETY

Every society, including our own, has been partial to games of chance. Whether it is betting on horseracing, buying a lottery ticket, or gambling in a casino, the opportunity to win, rather than earn, money has proved attractive for centuries. Eighteenth-century Londoners could play a national lottery, with tickets being insured and resold despite this being illegal. Street gambling, whether on early forms of roulette wheels or simply games of 'pitch and toss' were closed down regularly by the New Police from 1829, but this hardly dampened the enthusiasm for them. Londoners, it seems, have always loved 'a flutter'.

The elite practised an extreme form of gambling which helped establish some very significant and famous clubs in the capital. William Crockford was an illiterate fishmonger but canny enough with his investments to open a club in St James's where the rich and famous could gamble all night at hazard and other card games. At Crockford's, and clubs such as Almack's (later Boodle's), Brooks's, and White's, men and women won or more often lost hundreds of pounds.

In 1770 one young nobleman managed to lose £11,000 in an evening (close to £1.7 million today) and many were ruined as a consequence of their addiction to gambling. Sadly, some of those unable to face the shame associated with such losses chose to end their own lives. Membership of Almack's was by ballot, and any member could block a prospective entrant by selecting a black ball – which gives us the term 'blackballed'.

→ Drawing of the state lottery at the Guildhall, 1751.

DR GRAHAM AND HIS CELESTIAL BED
A CURIOUS CONTRAPTION TO AID CONCEPTION

↑ A suitably alluring image of a client trying out Dr Graham's infamous aid to reproduction.

A visitor to the Temple of Health, or from 1781, the more colourfully entitled Temple of Prolific Hymen at Schomberg House on fashionable Pall Mall, might have witnessed a demonstration of 'Dr' James Graham's 'Celestial Bed'. Graham was a self-styled (as he had no medical degree) sexologist, who published papers on reproduction. He opened his Temple of Health in 1780, having spent two years repurposing the smart London building into a sort of clinic offering all sorts of strange cures for everyday ailments. Here one could pay to hear Graham's diagnosis, purchase his medicines, experience music therapy and even bathe in mud.

But it was for his advice on sex, and particularly impotence, that Graham was most famous. Given the limited understanding of human reproduction in the late 1700s anything that might help a couple conceive a child was useful, especially to elite society with its obsession with continuing a lineage. To this end Graham had invented a contraption that he promised would aid conception. His Celestial Bed was twelve feet long by nine feet wide and was supported on 'pillars of brilliant glass'. It utilised the new science of electricity to create electromagnets for the stimulation of both partners. In addition, the bed could be tilted so that a man 'could follow his lady down-hill', to aid conception. Large audiences paid two guineas entry to watch his demonstrations, although presumably without active participants! Despite vigorous self-promotion, Graham made no money from his invention and died in 1794, a penniless lunatic.

ANIMAL CRUELTY IN LONDON
BETTING ON BLOOD SPORTS

Even in the 1800s the British love of animals ensured that there was a strong trade in pet food (sold by 'cat's meat' men), and in pets themselves. Londoners kept cats and dogs, budgies and canaries and, seemingly, a menagerie of other creatures. But the desire for non-human companionship did not prevent animals from being mistreated and abused. William Hogarth's print series 'On Cruelty' illustrates the casual violence meted out to horses, cats and dogs.

By the mid 1700s bull- and bear-baiting had largely disappeared, although dancing bears (with their handlers from the European continent) attracted crowds as late as the 1880s. Cockfighting survived well into the 1800s, despite it being made illegal, and 'ratting' (where sacks of rats were emptied into a pit for a dog to catch and kill) drew bloodthirsty audiences to pubs like the Blue Anchor in Bunhill Row. Attempts to supress blood sports were often as much about the associated gambling as the inherent cruelty. Until Smithfield changed from a 'live' to a 'dead' meat market in the 1860s, groups of youths would terrorise bullocks and then 'run' (chase) them through the streets, scattering pedestrians and upsetting carts and market stalls.

Eventually, 1824 saw the establishment of a campaign group dedicated to protecting animals, and thereafter officers of the SPCA (Society for the Prevention of Cruelty to Animals) were frequent visitors to the capital's police courts, bringing charges against cab drivers and coachmen who mistreated their horses, and owners who used excessive violence against their pets.

↑ The trial of Bill Burns, accused of beating his donkey, the world's first known conviction for animal cruelty.

← A cock fight in a London pub, an illustration by Thomas Rowlandson, 1808.

↑ The second of Hogarth's 'Four Stages of Cruelty'. A horse and sheep are beaten, while a bullock is chased.

HARRIS'S LIST OF COVENT GARDEN LADIES

A USEFUL GUIDE FOR THE LASCIVIOUS

While one could find a prostitute anywhere in eighteenth-century London, the epicentre of the trade was Covent Garden. From 1757 to 1795 a gazetteer listing between 150 and 190 'women of the town' offering sex for money provided a useful guide for the curious sex tourist. *Harris's List of Covent Garden Ladies or Men of Pleasure's Kalendar*, possibly inspired by a contemporary pimp, Jack Harris, gave readers details of the various 'ladies' available.

A description was given, along with a guide price, location (often a brothel) and, sometimes, even a guide to which sexual practices one might expect to receive. Names were carefully disguised, although anyone familiar with the trade would have easily recognised them. So, Mrs R__b__s__n of Carrington Street, (22), was described as 'elegant in her figure', and said to trade 'entirely on her *own bottom*'. She was supposedly available for both a 'flying skirmish' or a 'whole night's siege'! Several of the 'ladies' were listed as having keepers, wealthy men that set them up in lodgings, and who clothed and treated them as mistresses. This sometimes, but not always, meant that they were unavailable to other clients.

We can't be sure who wrote and published the 'List' but the name of Samuel Derrick, a Grub Street 'hack' (or journalist) is generally attributed to them. It sold very well, as many as 8,000 copies a year, and by the time it was effectively closed down in 1795 it was most likely being used as erotica by those that purchased it.

DR JOHN ST JOHN LONG

IT IS THE FATE OF MOST MEN TO HAVE MANY ENEMIES…

Visitors to Kensal Green Cemetery may notice a memorial which carries a message from beyond the grave! The domed monument is decorated with medical symbolism framing the following inscription: 'It is the fate of most men to have many enemies, and few friends'. It adds that the inhabitant 'was respected by those who knew his worth and the benefits derived from his remedial discovery'.

The tomb belongs to John St John Long (1798–1834) a quack doctor, who claimed to have found a cure for tuberculosis. Long, born in Ireland, set up in practice in London in 1822 and established himself in Harley Street in 1827. It all began to go wrong for 'Dr' Long in 1830 when, after treating Ellen Cashin for TB, he persuaded her mother to let him apply his techniques to her older daughter, Catherine. There was no evidence that Catharine had TB but Mrs Cashin agreed.

As a result of an incision Long made becoming infected, Catherine fell ill and, despite another doctor being called to help, she died. Long was tried for manslaughter at the Old Bailey, where he tried to blame the other medical man's interference, but he was convicted and fined £250 (maybe £24,000 today). He was acquitted of a similar case a month later. Ironically, Long may have himself succumbed to TB and it is said he refused his own treatment, dying in July 1834. However, it is possible he suffered a fall from a horse which caused his death aged thirty-six.

→ A satirical print shows 'Dr' Long surrounded by ducks: a very visual pun on 'quackery'.

DENS OF VICE & INIQUITY

PROSTITUTION
THE GREAT SOCIAL EVIL

Throughout the 1700s London's prostitutes had plied their trade with relatively little state interference. There were periodic clampdowns on 'disorderly women' picked up on the street by the night watch for annoying respectable passers-by, or for simply being rowdily drunk. There were attempts to suppress the sex trade: the 1752 Disorderly Houses Act (**see page 136**) targeted bawdy houses (brothels), and the Reformation of Manners movement encouraged magistrates to prosecute using the vagrancy laws. But 'prostitution' did not feature in legislation until the 1822 Vagrancy Act. This stipulated that 'Prostitutes or Night Walkers' were liable to a month in prison with hard labour if found on the street without being able to give a satisfactory account of themselves.

Yet while prostitution certainly exercised opinion in the eighteenth century it was from the 1840s that the female prostitute (male sex workers were rarely discussed) became the focus of moral scrutiny and a symbol of all female vice. While men were the clients of sex workers it was women who were deemed to be the problem. Estimates of the scale of the issue varied but in 1859 it was reported that 8,600 prostitutes were 'known to the police' and that the capital had 2,828 brothels. There were hundreds of women selling sex in poor areas like Whitechapel and Lambeth, but the spotlight often fell on prosperous places in the West End, like Regent Street and the Haymarket, where 'fallen women' might tempt gentlemen enjoying the theatre or their clubs.

In 1857 William Acton published a serious scientific study of prostitution which shocked his readership. From this point commentators began to use the phrase 'Great Social Evil' to refer to prostitution, reflecting the multiple concerns it posed for Victorian society. For some it was the fate of the women, often young girls, that mattered: from the 1700s there had been the trope of the exploited serving girl like Hogarth's 'Moll Hackabout' who arrived as an innocent in the metropolis only to be corrupted and forced into prostitution. This persisted in the 1800s but was sometimes eclipsed by the view that sex workers spread diseases like syphilis and gonorrhoea, which had a debilitating effect on society, and, in the aftermath of the Crimean War, the men that defended the empire. In 1864, Parliament passed the first of three Contagious Diseases Acts which, while not implemented in the capital, targeted streetwalkers in garrison and port towns with forced examination and treatment for STIs, effectively regulating the trade until their repeal in 1886.

Prostitution reared its head again in 1888 as a number of 'unfortunates' were butchered by Jack the Ripper (**see page 30**), just after efforts by reformers had persuaded Parliament to pass the Criminal Law Amendment Act (1885) which, among other things (**see page 114**) closed brothels forcing women onto the streets. At the end of the century the Moral Purity movement continued to promote chastity and rail against the sex trade, but attempts to supress it via the law continued to be ineffective.

← A scene from William Hogarth's 'A Harlot's Progress'. A procureress (right) meets an innocent country girl just arrived in London, and leads her into a life of prostitution, disease and death.

MACARONIS

DEDICATED FOLLOWERS OF FASHION

Youth fashions are nothing new, whether it be Punks or New Romantics, Mods and Rockers in the 1960s, or Teddy Boys in the 1950s, young men and women have enjoyed pushing the boundaries of taste to shock older generations and to create identities of their own. It would seem that this was as true in the 1700s as it remains today.

The 1760s saw the emergence of a variety of male (and later female) fashion that would later shape the mainstream. Wealthy young men, often those who'd undertaken the European Tour and who enjoyed a night's gambling at a club like Almack's (**see page 122**) adopted a colourful and extravagant dress code which was at odds with the sombre one generally preferred by men in Georgian London. With bright silks, short coats, big hair (or wigs) and ribbons, the look was undoubtedly more feminine than regular contemporary male fashion.

The proponents of this look were dubbed 'macaronis', in reference to the Italian foodstuff which was seen as exotic and new, and because foreign (i.e. French and Italian) clothes were considered more fashionable and desirable. The members of the Macaroni club patronised the arts but perhaps only as an affectation; their main pursuit was pleasure and so they earned an unwelcome reputation as the epitome of aristocratic excess and degeneracy. By the 1770s women were aping the fashion with teetering wigs and headdresses, and it was evident that the 'macaroni' look was being adopted more widely, which ended its appeal to trendsetters.

← Satirical print depicting a Macaroni.

FREDERICK PARK AND ERNEST BOULTON
FANNY AND STELLA GO TO COURT

We might see the Victorian period as strait-laced and repressed but it was often very far from that, and closer to our own world than we might imagine. In the 1860s a touring theatrical troupe had entertained audiences with a show that included two men dressed as women. Fanny (Frederick William Park) and Stella (Thomas Ernest Boulton) appeared on stage and off as women, and in 1870 this led to them being arrested. They were charged with 'buggery' and 'openly and scandalously' outraging and corrupting public morals.

These were serious crimes, even if sodomy no longer carried the death penalty, as it had until 1861. Having been arrested as they left the Strand Theatre the pair appeared at Bow Street Police Court dressed in female attire, which drew large crowds. They were submitted to internal physical examination and held for two months on remand before their trial commenced at Queen's Bench in 1871.

Fanny and Stella were tried with three others but the police could offer no conclusive proof that any of them had engaged in illegal forms of sexual intercourse and they were all acquitted. The jury did find Boulton and Park guilty of cross-dressing in public and in so doing committing 'an offence against public morals and common decency', for which they were bound over for two years. Crowds of well-wishers cheered when the not-guilty verdict was delivered, a reminder that some parts of society had no problem with these pioneers of sexual freedom.

← A photograph of Fanny (right) and Stella (left) taken less than a year before their arrest.

DENS OF VICE & INIQUITY

← Stella and Fanny are escorted into a 'Black Maria' (police vehicle) as they are taken into custody.

DENS OF VICE & INIQUITY

DISORDERLY HOUSES ACT 1752

FUTILE ATTEMPTS TO SUPRESS BROTHELS

The start of the 1750s saw something of a moral panic about crime and immorality. A Parliamentary committee was established to investigate and told, by several London magistrates, that there were simply too many places where people could be tempted into vice and 'riotous pleasures'. This led to the Disorderly Houses Act in 1752 which required premises offering entertainment to be licensed. A venue without one was deemed to be 'disorderly' and was liable to be raided by the parish constabulary.

The legislation applied widely but was designed to target brothels (aka 'bawdy houses') where known prostitutes operated. Rewards were offered to informants, and financial penalties were served on constables who failed to act. This, and a rather loose definition of what or whom an 'owner' of a bawdy house was, were designed to support the closing down of brothels in London. Regardless of the evident determination of some sections of society, the legislation does not seem to have made much difference at all. Bawdy houses continued to serve their clients, most likely because brothel madams and pimps made sure to bribe the right people.

Indeed almost one hundred years later police were still trying to enforce the act, as a case from 1849 reveals. Two women, Elizabeth Berkeley and Susanna Skudder (aka Susanna Wood), were charged with keeping a bawdy house on Rupert Street. PC Joseph Allen from Leman Street police station gave evidence the brothel was still operating, despite several attempts to close it down.

← Two prostitutes bribe a doorman to turn a blind eye to their activities. West End clubs and hotels were a profitable hunting ground for nineteenth-century sex workers.

→ A woman is brought in to the Great Marlborough Street police court for 'loitering' in the streets.

"FOR PRISONERS ONLY".

PUNISHMENT OF ANN MARROW

BLINDED IN THE PILLORY FOR MARRYING THREE WOMEN

In July 1777, a number of London newspapers reported the conviction of a woman for 'going in men's cloaths [sic], and being married to three different women by a fictitious name'. Her sentence was three months' imprisonment and to be made to stand in the pillory at Charing Cross. The pillory was an instrument of punishment (**see page 17**) which allowed the public to participate in the ritual humiliation of those who had been found guilty of transgressing laws or social norms, and the treatment meted out there could be brutal.

In this case the pillory's 'victim' was Ann Marrow (aka Marlow, Marhow and Marrish). She had been prosecuted by George Field at the Westminster Quarter Sessions accused of a fraud, which appears to have been impersonating a man and then taking money from each of the young women she had married. She may have used the name 'Charles' for her alternate identity, and we could see Ann/Charles as an early pioneer of single-sex marriages.

The crowd that gathered at Charing Cross was hostile and reported to have been 'several thousand strong'. A woman in the pillory was a spectacle that might be expected to draw plenty of curious and mawkish onlookers, but what happened to Ann was not normal. The mob turned on her, abusing her verbally and physically to the extent that she was taken away so badly injured her life was in the balance. She survived but lost the sight in both her eyes.

THE 1822 VAGRANCY ACT

A FUTILE ATTEMPT TO SUPPRESS PROSTITUTION

Prior to 1822, 'prostitute' was not commonly used in legal terminology. The Vagrancy Act of that year changed that. The legislation, formally entitled 'An Act for Consolidating into one Act and Amending the Laws relating to Idle and Disorderly Persons, Rogues and Vagabonds', both specifically named prostitutes and included clauses to deal with them. Thereafter, any woman found on the streets at night unable to explain, to the satisfaction of the officer who stopped them, why they were there, could be arrested and charged as idle and disorderly. If found guilty they faced up to a month in a house of correction (**see page 70**).

The impact of the law was limited; arrests rose slightly before settling down again. It was replaced in 1824 by a new Vagrancy Act under which women could be arrested for simply 'wandering and behaving in a riotous or indecent manner'. It was an admission that attempting to supress prostitution was a futile endeavour, as countless law enforcement agencies had recognised previously (and indeed since).

Police gained an additional weapon in 1839: section 54 (II) of the Metropolitan Police Act criminalised soliciting for prostitution. Even this was problematic though, as the Police Code Book acknowledged. Prosecution relied on complaints being made by the men whom the women approached and, perhaps understandably, most were unwilling to appear in court to uphold them.

→ An awkward encounter as a flower seller (perhaps using this as a ruse to solicit prostitution) attracts the unwanted attention of her client's wife.

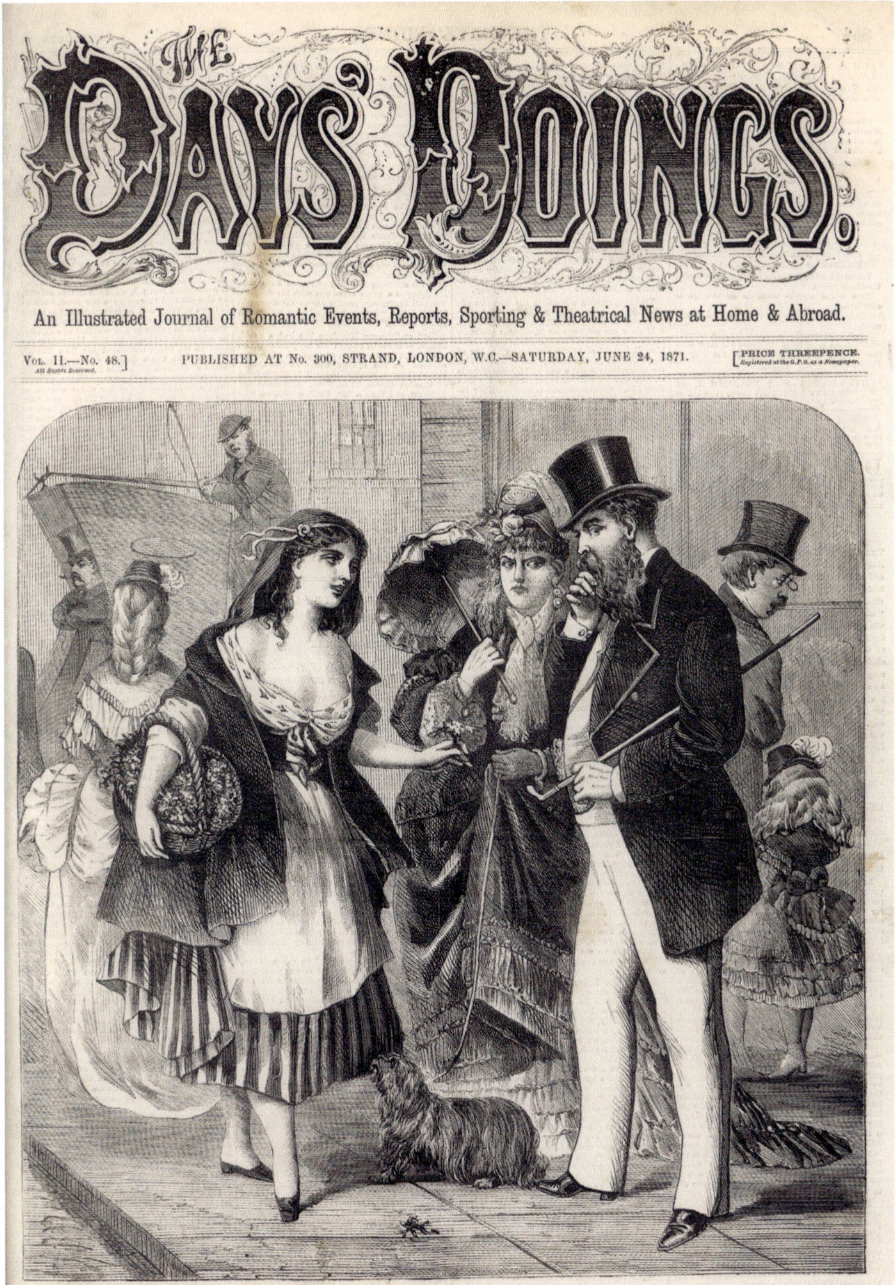

AWKWARD CONTRE-TEMPS IN REGENT STREET DURING THE HEIGHT OF THE SEASON.
"That Girl seems to know you, George!"

DENS OF VICE & INIQUITY

THE CHEVALIÈR D'ÉON

THE FIRST OPENLY TRANSGENDER CELEBRITY?

MAD.^{lle} LA CHEVALIERE D'EON DE BEAUMONT
Fencing at Carlton House, 9th April 1787.

Charles d'Éon was born in 1728 into a lowly but noble French family. D'Éon pursued a career as a political writer which helped him find employment with the French government as a censor. D'Éon was then recruited into the state's spy network before serving as a captain of Dragoons in the Seven Years War (1756–63).

None of this would set d'Éon apart as particularly interesting if it were not for the fact that by the time the Chevalièr d'Éon was settled in residence in London (1875), they had become Charlotte, not Charles. While it isn't clear how d'Éon would have described their gender it is reasonably well documented that they lived in London as a woman, not a man. Charlotte d'Éon became a well-known member of Georgian high society and, more remarkably, gave performances of sword fighting in an age when it would have been highly unusual for women to practise fencing, let alone to do so publicly.

Speculation about d'Éon's gender had been rife since the 1770s at least, with wagers being made at the London Stock Exchange. Chevalièr d'Éon had even asked the French government to recognise that they had been born female, not male. Louis XVI allowed d'Éon to dress as a woman, something they seem to have done consistently from the 1770s. When d'Éon died in 1810, impoverished in London, the surgeon performing an autopsy observed that they possessed male genitalia but also 'female characteristics'. It would seem Charles/Charlotte was centuries ahead of their time.

↑ The Chevalièr gives a demonstration of fencing.

HENRY SPENCER ASHBEE

WAS HE 'WALTER'?

Henry Ashbee was, like many educated and well-travelled Victorian men, an avid collector of books, pamphlets, art and antiquities. Indeed, the British Museum and the Victoria & Albert Museum were both beneficiaries of bequests from Ashbee's estate following his death in 1900. Ashbee is most famous however, for his collection of erotica, and a three-volume bibliography of erotic literature which he published under the pseudonym 'Pisanus Fraxi', a suitably erudite play on his surname.

It is also possible (though not conclusively proven) that Ashbee was the author of *My Secret Life*, using the alter ego 'Walter'. *My Secret Life* is the memoir of a Victorian gentleman's sexual indulgences in the capital, and most especially London's numerous brothels and what he found there. The print edition ran to eleven volumes but had a limited print run for each. 'Walter' begins his story by reminiscing about his childhood, and what might seem to us to be abuse at the hands of a nursemaid. The work is filled with his encounters with women, most of whom are either prostitutes or servants, so it is a memoir of his activities outside of his social class.

In terms of literature, it is not generally viewed as being of much merit but as a social and cultural document it certainly has some value to historians. If it wasn't written by Ashbee, and instead by one of the handful of others suggested by experts, then it is likely that he knew or suspected who had penned it.

← Henry Ashbee from a contemporary photograph.

DENS OF VICE & INIQUITY   141

DISASTERS & DESTITUTION

THE ST GILES ROOKERY

THE HAUNT OF THE DRUNKARD AND THE DEBAUCHEE

Eighteenth and nineteenth-century London had pockets of poverty and deprivation that were deemed so extreme that even policemen avoided entering them. They were dubbed 'rookeries', presumably because of their resemblance to the nests of corvids.

Charles Dickens described the area around Seven Dials as 'filthy and miserable', a community of the poor and criminal living in dilapidated houses, long abandoned by wealthy Londoners who had moved out of the centre as the city grew. One correspondent, writing in 1843, just as the St Giles Rookery was about to be demolished, recorded that the area 'had long been the haunt of the drunkard and the debauchee'. Dickens noted the large number of gin houses selling the cheap liquor that the capital's poorest imbibed to numb the misery of their short lives. This is where Hogarth set *Gin Lane* in 1751 with its powerful image of callous neglect and degradation (**see page 182**).

The St Giles Rookery was dubbed 'Little Ireland' because so many of its inhabitants were migrants, or the descendants of migrants from the Emerald Isle, and widely held negative perceptions of the Irish as drunks and thieves appeared to be proved true by anyone visiting St Giles. With its densely packed houses, narrow alleyways, rotten floors and traps set for any unwary policemen who ventured in, the rookery of St Giles was a cancer at the heart of the metropolis.

← The St Giles Rookery was synonymous with poverty, drunkenness, degradation and crime.

GAOL FEVER

A PESTILENT DISEASE, WHICH IS CALLED THE GAOL DISTEMPER

In 1750 an outbreak of 'gaol fever' at Newgate Prison killed dozens of prisoners. More importantly (to the authorities at least) it also claimed four judges, some lawyers, a number of jurors, the under sheriff for Middlesex and about thirty others attending the adjacent Old Bailey courtroom. Prisoners died of fever all the time, but the deaths of members of the elite and 'middling sorts' forced the City to launch an enquiry.

The findings were not news to anyone familiar with Newgate but were shocking nevertheless. Chronic overcrowding, insanitary conditions, the miserable physical state of the inmates and poor ventilation were all highlighted. A report recommended improved ventilation, clean water and the routine cleansing, or even burning of prisoners' lice-infested clothing. As a ventilator was being checked an apprentice fell into the shaft (apparently while trying to retrieve a wig dropped by his master) and fell ill complaining of 'a violent head-ache, [and] a great disorder in his stomach'.

Gaol fever is better known to modern science as typhus, an epidemic louse-born disease which causes headaches, fever, swollen lymph nodes, skin rash, nausea and vomiting. Untreated it can be fatal, as it was to many in the 1700s and 1800s. There were periodic outbreaks of typhus at Newgate and the problem was not really solved until the mid-Victorian age, when prison reform was firmly established and the chaos of places like Newgate was substituted for the order and control of Pentonville.

← Prisoners' clothes are fumigated at Coldbath Fields Prison to kill the lice that spread diseases.

THE TOTTENHAM COURT ROAD GAS EXPLOSION
I FELT THE GROUND SHAKING...

In the early evening of 5 July 1880, workmen were finishing off alterations to a gas supply pipe on Percy Street, close to Tottenham Court Road. One of the men was holding a naked flame to examine the work and within seconds there was a massive explosion. This was followed by subsequent blasts which ripped up several streets and sent debris flying in all directions, smashing into windows and over rooftops.

An eyewitness walking on Percy Street said he felt 'the ground shaking under my feet' before the blast knocked him over and into a cavity caused by the street's collapse. A horse and cart were thrown up in the air by the explosion before falling into the cavern that had opened in nearby Charlotte Street. Several children who had been playing in the street had to be helped out of a hole, and there were many similar stories. A performance at the nearby Prince of Wales Theatre was suspended as the gas supply was cut off.

In total more than 400 properties in a half-mile vicinity were damaged, with dozens of people being hurt. The fire brigade and police rushed to the scene and began to help the injured. William Burr, the man whose light caused the explosion, was so badly mutilated that he 'presented a fearful spectacle' when he was taken to the Middlesex Hospital. He died of his wounds the following day. Alfred Davis also died from multiple fractures and the shock to his system.

↑ Dramatic newspaper coverage of the Tottenham Court Road explosion.

THE METYARDS

A MOTHER AND DAUGHTER UNITED IN CRUELTY

The mistreatment of apprentices was certainly not uncommon. Dickens didn't have to invent Oliver Twist's tormentors; there was plenty of evidence for their existence. Routine beatings and back-breaking days of work were one thing, but outright cruelty and murder were less common.

On 19 July 1768, Sarah Metyard and her daughter, Sarah Morgan, were hanged at Tyburn for killing a young apprentice, Ann Nailor, and also, in all probability, murdering her eight-year-old sister. The Metyards were milliners who took in apprentices supplied by various London workhouses, and they treated them abominably. In 1758, Ann and her sister Mary were so badly abused that Ann tried to run away. Caught by the milkman she was dragged upstairs, beaten with a broom handle, tied up and denied food.

Within days she was found slumped and insensible; Ann had died, and so the Metyards tried to cover it up. They stored her body in a box in the attic and claimed she'd run away. As the body putrefied and began to stink, mother and daughter chopped it up and carried it to the Chick Lane 'gulley-hole' (a manhole cover over the drains) to dispose of it. It didn't take long for the body to surface but it was years before the women were brought to justice. At their trial, daughter turned on mother in a desperate if futile attempt to save her own neck. Both went to the gallows and their bodies were afterwards dissected at Surgeons' Hall (**see page 110**).

← The Metyards chop up Ann's body while their cat looks on, possibly the artist's attempt to associate the pair with witchcraft.

DISASTERS & DESTITUTION   147

TOTTIE FAY AGAIN!
ALCOHOLISM IN LATE VICTORIAN LONDON

In 1898 Parliament legislated to recognise alcoholism as a medically treatable condition. That this change happened is in part due to the experience of a handful of infamous characters, the most notable of whom was 'Tottie Fay'. Fay was a pseudonym, one of dozens adopted by Amy Anderson, who became a minor newspaper celebrity. Born in Seven Dials, Anderson was determined to escape the poverty of where she grew up.

Her playbook was straightforward; she would pick up men as they turned out of West End theatres and clubs, and persuade them to treat her to a drink. Then, bribing a hotel porter, she'd supply sex in comfortable surroundings. Sadly, she became reliant on alcohol and less able to attract custom. On multiple occasions, Tottie appeared in court charged with drunk and disorderly behaviour and, occasionally, more serious crimes. She'd be fined and, as she rarely had the funds to pay the fines, sent to prison.

Frequent court appearances and more serious offences such as theft and fraud meant longer spells behind bars. The press delighted in reporting her eccentric appearances, her bizarre clothing choices and multiple aliases. Then in 1892 she was sent down for three years and transferred to Broadmoor as 'insane'. At the time of her death in 1908 she'd been in and out of several institutions for alcohol-induced insanity.

There were others like Tottie, and the revolving cycle of drunkenness-arrest-court-prison-release-drunkenness helped convince MPs that something had to be done. The 1898 Inebriates Act allowed alcoholics to be sent to institutions to dry out and get some help, however limited. A register of those released was established, with photographs to warn publicans not to serve them, and so policemen could keep an eye on them.

← Tottie Fay 'dances' on the front cover of *The Illustrated Police News*.

THE PRINCESS ALICE DISASTER

A FAMILY DAY OUT ENDS IN TRAGEDY

On the evening of 3 September 1878, the SS *Princess Alice*, a paddle steamer carrying hundreds of passengers returning from a day trip, was making its way up the Thames near Woolwich. As the *Alice* turned into Gallions Reach another, larger vessel – the *Bywell Castle*, a steam-powered cargo liner – was occupying the same river channel.

At this time there were no rules about which side of the Thames vessels should use, although this would change as a result of what happened on this fateful day. Despite the efforts of both crews the ships collided. The *Princess Alice* was cut open, quickly split apart, and sank. The crew of the *Bywell Castle* promptly threw out ropes and launched all their lifeboats, an action that saved around sixty lives. But ten times that number drowned. The catastrophe was made even worse because of the polluted state of the Thames at that particular location, as the sewage pumping station at Barking Reach emptied many tonnes of effluent into the water.

Bodies washed up for several days afterwards, and the wreck of the *Princess Alice* was an eerie graveyard to those who had become trapped inside it. In total 640 people died, many without their names ever being recorded. A Board of Trade inquiry exonerated the captain and crew of the *Bywell Castle*, and instead placed the blame squarely on the other vessel. The coroner's inquest was more even-handed. The result was that 'proper and stringent rules and regulations [were] laid down for all stream navigation on the River Thames' from that point on.

← Recovering the dead from the Thames after the *Princess Alice* disaster.

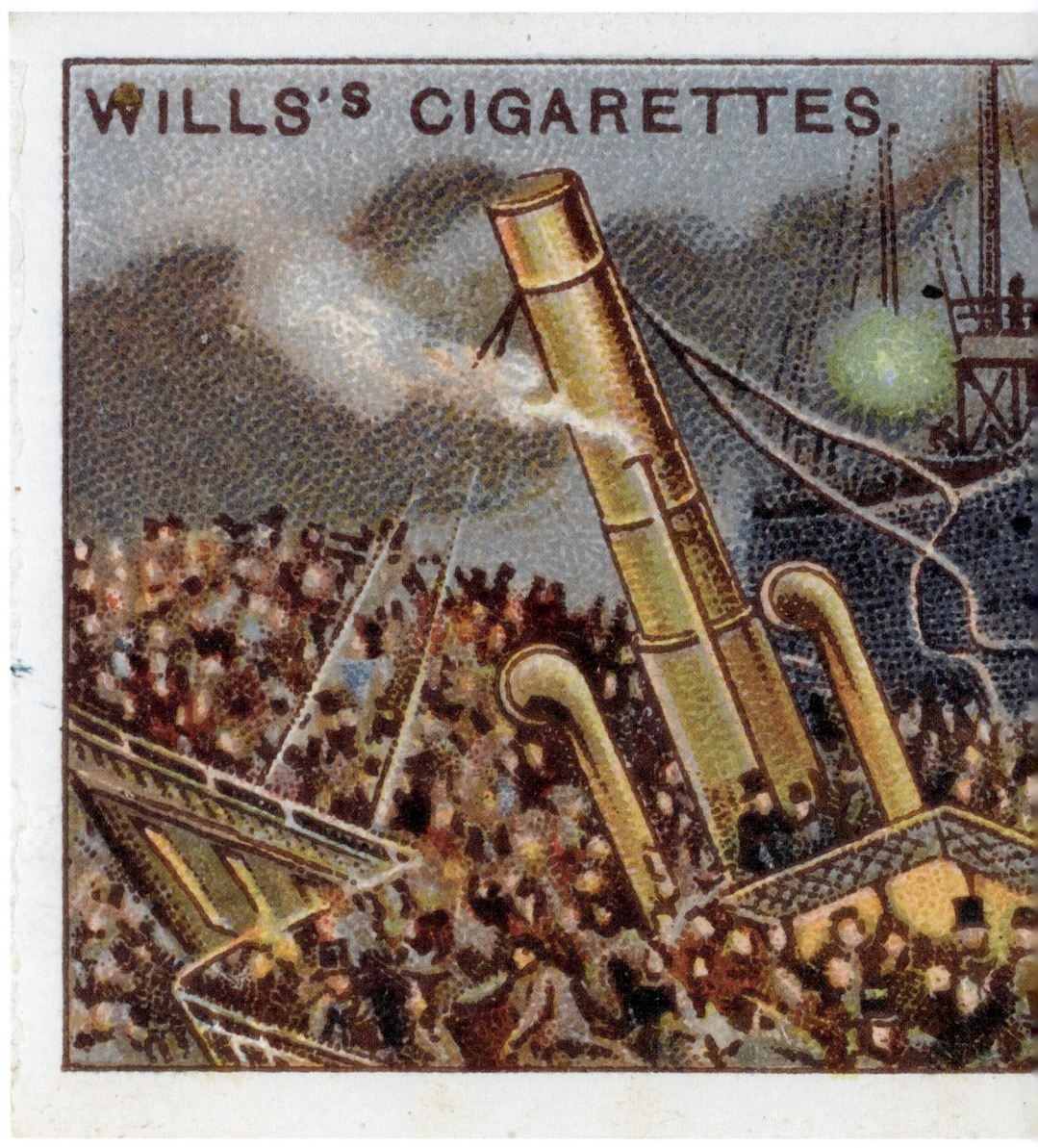

↑ The disaster became part of the popular culture of the late Victorian period, as this cigarette card illustration shows.

DISASTERS & DESTITUTION 151

THE BEER FLOOD
ST GILES AWASH WITH A TIDE OF BEER

On 14 October 1814, an accident at the Horseshoe Brewery in central London caused the death of eight people and damaged or destroyed property in the vicinity of the overcrowded St Giles Rookery (**see page 144**). A clerk at the brewery told the coroner's inquest that he saw one of the iron hoops round a vat burst off around 4.30 in the afternoon. This was not unknown and he wrote to his employers to tell them about it, but an hour later, the whole vat burst and he found himself up to his knees in London porter (a stout beer).

The rapid escape of 320,000 gallons of liquid not only flooded the brewery, but it also broke down the walls of the building and spilled into the area beyond. This tide of beer flooded two nearby cellars, in one of which a family was holding a wake for an infant. Tragedy piled on tragedy as all the mourners were crushed or drowned.

Among the dead was Eleanor Cooper, a servant at the Tavistock Arms on Great Russell Street. She had been washing pots in the yard when the wave brought down part of the building and trapped her under the rubble. The flood also claimed the lives of three children and two elderly widows. In the days that followed, Londoners came to view the wreckage of the brewery, with local watchmen charging a penny or two for the chance to get close to the ruins, despite the danger of further collapses.

BILLS OF MORTALITY
A WEEKLY LOOK AT WHAT AILED US

Until the introduction of Medical Officer of Health Reports in the mid 1800s, and annual reports from the Registrar General, Bills of Mortality provided the best available guide to the causes of death in London. From the late 1500s, these one-page weekly bulletins of death listed the numbers of Londoners who had fatally succumbed to disease, accident, or self-inflicted injury. They also listed christenings and burials and made comparisons with the previous week.

The Bills are, therefore, a fascinating window into what killed our ancestors. Not surprisingly, 1665 was a particularly bad year, the plague killing 68,596 people, including 8,000 souls in just one week in September. By the 1800s 'plague' no longer featured but plenty of other curious entries warrant attention. It will come as no surprise that 'age and debility' were the cause of death for forty Londoners who died in the week ending 13 September 1836. They were joined by twenty-nine who suffered 'convulsions', as well as seven who died of 'Dropsy on the brain'. Many others were taken by 'consumption' (tuberculosis), some by 'inflammation' (of the lungs, brain, bowel, or stomach), plus liver disease, measles, apoplexy and asthma.

Childbirth claimed six women, and eight people died as a result of 'dentition or teething'. Some of the latter might have been babies and, overall, the statistics for that week in 1836 reveal that 183 males and 163 females were buried across London's 130 parishes. By contrast, London's vicars christened 282 male children and 237 baby girls.

→ Burying the dead in the plague of 1665.

THE REGENT'S PARK SKATING DISASTER

SUCH A SIGHT I HOPE
NEVER TO SEE AGAIN

People of all ages in Victorian London enjoyed the opportunities for fun that the capital's many parks provided. In 1867 this passion for the outdoors ended in tragedy as forty-one people lost their lives in the worst skating disaster the country has ever known. It happened on 16 January, as hundreds gathered at a frozen lake in Regent's Park. Some were skating on the ice, others jumping onto the ice from the sides of the lake, while a group of men were also engaged in a vigorous hockey match.

Then at about 4.15 in the afternoon the ice suddenly gave way, plunging 200 or more people into freezing water. Shocked by the cold and encumbered by heavy clothing, many went under and struggled to reach safety. There were heroes that day: one man spent an hour helping others before he was eventually rescued by a pleasure boat. The disaster was, like that of the *Princess Alice* on the Thames in 1878 (**see page 149**), no respecter of social class. The icy waters of the lake claimed the lives of wealthy men and their wives, while also taking working men like James Griffin, a twenty-nine-year-old from Drury Lane who had been selling oranges to the revellers before the ice broke beneath him.

Those saved by the lifeguards in the employ of the Royal Humane Society, and by impromptu boat crews, were taken to the St Marylebone Infirmary and St Mary's Hospital in Paddington; the dead were laid out at the nearest workhouse.

→ Rescue boats desperately try to reach survivors in the icy water.

DISASTERS & DESTITUTION 155

← A view of the torrent of water as it flooded the tunnel, from *The Finish to the Adventures of Tom, Jerry and Logic*, 1828.

THE THAMES TUNNEL

A NARROW ESCAPE FOR
A GREAT ENGINEER

In 1825, Marc Brunel began work on an ambitious project to build a tunnel under the River Thames, to provide a railway cargo line between Rotherhithe and Wapping. The necessity of building a tunnel so close to the river bed meant that those working on the project, including Brunel's son Isambard, were horribly exposed to the risks of flooding.

In 1828, and only days after Marc Brunel had escorted the heir to the Portuguese throne around the works, disaster struck. As evening fell the weight of mud broke open the shaft and the river poured in. Some workers were crushed instantly, others drowned soon afterwards despite the efforts of colleagues to save them. Isambard Kingdom Brunel was trapped in the flooding, narrowly escaping death and displaying great heroism attempting to save lives. He would return to the tunnel day after day, using a diving bell to assess the damage, continuing to work regardless of the injuries he sustained.

Six men lost their lives in what was just one of several collapses during construction. Thomas Ball, John Collins and John Long all left grieving widows, and Jeptha Cooke's six children were made orphans by the tragedy. The other deceased workers were Thomas Evans and William Seton. It took many more years before the tunnel finally opened in 1843. By then its purpose had changed; no longer a cargo route, instead it served pedestrians until 1869 when it was sold to the London Metropolitan Railway as a ventilation shaft for the London Underground, or 'tube'.

RIOTS IN TRAFALGAR SQUARE

BLOODY SUNDAY 1887

A severe economic downturn in the 1880s brought thousands of Londoners onto the city's streets protesting at their lack of work and demanding action to protect prices and the home economy. Trafalgar Square would become the central focus of protest. Groups demanding the government create jobs by initiating great public works, or placing restrictions on foreign imports, were joined by unemployed dockers and small manufacturing workers from the East End.

In February 1886, a demonstration by the Fair Trade League clashed with another called by the Social Democratic Federation (a socialist party led by Henry Hyndman), and inept policing allowed a section of the crowd to move off into the West End where they attacked shops and wealthy clubs on Pall Mall. The 'West End' riots prompted the resignation of the Metropolitan Police Commissioner whose replacement, Charles Warren, was determined that the police would not be caught by surprise again. In November 1887, after attempting to ban demonstrations in the square, Warren organised his officers on military lines and enlisted troops from the Life Guards to assist.

On 13 November the result was 'Bloody Sunday' when lines of police and red-coated cavalrymen charged protesters, breaking heads and tearing down placards and banners. The radical press derided the police as 'ruffians in uniform', while the establishment purred with pleasure at Warren's resolve. At least one man, Alfred Linnell, died that day and his funeral drew the largest mourning crowds London had seen since that of the Duke of Wellington.

DISASTERS & DESTITUTION

→ Protestors surge down Pall Mall in 1886; St James' Place is visible in the background.

EXPLOSION AT A FIREWORKS FACTORY
TWO GIRLS MANGLED BEYOND RECOGNITION

← The explosion rips through the firework factory.

Cadwell & Co.'s firework factory in Wandsworth manufactured the small paper percussion caps used to give toy pistols their realistic 'bang!'. The caps were made in the centre shed on their premises in Garrett Lane, which in 1888 stood in an area well removed from local housing. A chemical manure factory and a soap works were fairly close, as was the London & South Western railway station at Earlsfield.

The caps were made by women, and on 10 August 1888, sisters Eliza and Elizabeth Thornton were working alongside Lucy Horwood and Rose Sawyer on what was, seemingly at least, an average Friday. Then suddenly, and without a clear explanation, a dramatic explosion ripped the shed apart so that nothing remained but a few burning embers. When those startled by the noise ran to the scene, they discovered the Thornton sisters' bodies almost 'mangled beyond recognition'; both were dead, leaving their mother the only support for Mr Thornton, who had been invalided out of work years before.

The two other injured girls were taken to Wandsworth Infirmary where Lucy died of her injuries having had an arm amputated; Rose's injuries were serious but not life threatening. The factory owner and officials from the Home Office picked through the rubble to try to make sense of the accident. The caps on their own should not have caused such a blast, so it was suggested that another, more volatile material must have been brought into the shed.

HEBREW DRAMATIC CLUB STAMPEDE

SCREAMS OF TERROR IN WHITECHAPEL

In January 1887 an audience of 400 theatregoers were enjoying an evening of entertainment by amateur performers when disaster struck. At about 11 p.m. a gas leak and fire was reported, and moments later all the lights went out. Panic ensued: 'Screams of terror [...] cries of appeal and advice mingled', as hundreds surged for the exits of the Hebrew Dramatic Club on Prince's Street (now Princelet Street), Spitalfields.

In the rush, many were trampled or crushed against the doors and walls, dying of suffocation. Their bodies were examined by police surgeon George Bagster Phillips, who would later examine many of Jack the Ripper's victims. In total seventeen people, all members of the local Jewish community, were killed in the chaos. Funerals took place quickly, as is Jewish custom, and *The Jewish Chronicle* set up a subscription to help the bereaved. Spare a thought for Mr and Mrs Krotofsky of Pelham Street, who lost two teenage sons that evening, and the husband of Millie Gubert who lost his wife and twelve-year-old son Isaac.

The manager of the club, a butcher from Dorset Street named Smith, told the inquest that the fire warning was false, the stampede unnecessary, and that he'd done everything possible to ensure people could leave safely. The hall was a scene of devastation with the stage's footlights flattened by stamping boots and the venue strewn with abandoned costumes, clothing and even a baby's rattle, a poignant reminder that this was a disaster that impacted a whole community.

↑ An illustrator captures the destruction caused by theatregoers frantically fleeing from a false rumour of danger.

SUICIDE OF MARGARET MOYES
TRAGEDY AT THE MONUMENT

In 1677, Sir Christopher Wren and Dr Robert Hooke's design for a monument to commemorate the Great Fire of London was opened. Londoners were now able to climb 311 steps to the top to view the panorama of the rebuilt capital city below. Today, visitors to the summit are protected from falling by wire mesh, but this wasn't the case in the 1800s. In 1810 a Jewish diamond merchant named Levi threw himself off the Monument and, a year later, a baker from Reading also took his life in the same way.

But it was the suicide of a young woman called Margaret Moyes that caught the attention of the press in 1839. Margaret, the daughter of a master baker in Charing Cross, was described as 'fine and handsome'. She told the gatekeeper Thomas Jenkins she was waiting for some friends and handed him sixpence, the price of entry to the tower. Not long afterwards witnesses were shocked to see her falling from the top of the structure and colliding with a bird cage before she struck the ground. Jenkins raced up the tower to find her bonnet and a rope she'd used to pull herself up and over, tied to the railings.

Margaret was just twenty-two, her mother was dead and her father was terminally ill. Apparently, she'd left home early that morning, leaving a note declaring 'her family should never see her again'. The coroner concluded she suffered from 'temporary insanity' at the prospect of being left with no one to support her.

← The Monument, which marks the starting point of the Great Fire of London, has itself been witness to very personal tragedies.

THE 1824 VAGRANCY ACT

A CATCH-ALL LAW TO PENALISE THE HOMELESS

In June 1824, a new Vagrancy Act became law. This was a 'catch all' piece of legislation, and was heavily criticised as such by William Wilberforce, the anti-slavery campaigner. It granted the courts (and after 1829 the 'New Police') considerable powers to deal with anyone found on the streets who could not give a good account of themselves. It was drafted in the aftermath of the Napoleonic Wars (1803–1815) when returning servicemen swelled the ranks of the poor, amplifying well-established concerns about large numbers of homeless beggars and vagrants.

The act covered the 'idle and disorderly', 'incorrigible rogues' and 'vagabonds', and prescribed short periods of imprisonment and hard labour in Houses of Correction (**see page 70**) to deter repeat offenders. Missing from the legislation was any attempt to understand or ameliorate the condition of poverty that led to people taking to the streets in the first place. The act also targeted those who professed an ability to tell fortunes or organised games of chance (gambling) on the streets. From 1838, the act was also used against those selling obscene prints or books. Even the walking wounded, who tried to win sympathy by exposing their wounds or disabilities, were sanctioned by the Vagrancy Act.

In effect the act criminalised homelessness, and it has never been fully repealed, meaning hundreds of Londoners are still arrested under a 200-year-old statute.

↑ A policeman's lantern illuminates rough sleepers on the Embankment.

DISASTERS & DESTITUTION 163

THE WOOD GREEN RAILWAY CRASH

A TRAIN TURNS TURTLE

← The aftermath of the Wood Green crash, as one newspaper illustrator saw it.

The railways transformed Victorian Britain, opening up the country as never before by linking north to south, prompting migrations from rural areas to the capital's growing urban sprawl. Within London, railways allowed people to live further from their workplaces, initiating the development of the suburbs, and Londoners could also now enjoy trips to the seaside and other parts of the country. But the railways also brought problems: communities were scattered as stations like Liverpool Street were built, and newspapers were full of stories of 'outrages' in railway carriages, suicides on tracks and, inevitably, fatal accidents.

One of these occurred in March 1895, when a train arriving at Wood Green station on the Great Northern line snapped an axle and careered off the tracks. On this occasion the loss of life and injury was limited because the train was empty aside from its crew. When the train collided with the platform it 'turned turtle' (in other words, it was thrown up in the air and landed upside down), and the driver and fireman were trapped in the cab, and crushed by the weight of the metal.

Edward Cowland, the fireman, was killed instantly while the driver, Charles Floyd, lived a few hours longer. The guard had a lucky escape; his van was also overturned but while the wooden structure was smashed to pieces, he walked away largely unscathed. The station was closed for some time to the 'great inconvenience' of passengers, but the railway company quickly established an alternative service on the Enfield line.

THE WORKHOUSE IN LoNDON
BASTILLES FOR THE POOR

George W. Bacon's 1888 *New Large Scale Ordnance Atlas of London & Suburbs* lists no fewer than forty-five parish workhouses, from which we can safely conclude that anyone growing up in Victorian London was acutely aware of their existence. Workhouses had been a part of the landscape throughout the eighteenth century, especially after the passing of the Workhouse Test Act (1723). But it was under the new Poor Law that they achieved their status as places of dread in the hearts and minds of working-class Londoners.

The Poor Law Amendment Act that came into force in 1834 was intentionally crafted in order to deter paupers from seeking help unless they were absolutely desperate. Instead of outdoor relief such as doles (parish rates used to provide support during periods of unemployment or insufficient wages), those in need were now required to enter 'the house'. Therein they would be given workhouse clothing, families were separated, and everyone set to work for the meagre sustenance allowed. From 1846 'casual' wards were established and those entering could expect an even more punitive experience, as the journalist James Greenwood described when he spent a night in Lambeth's workhouse. Although he wrote of the overcrowding, the 'skilley' (oatmeal and water) he was given to eat, and the work (grinding corn) he was set to, he refrained from telling his readership about the 'horrors infinitely more revolting' he witnessed.

Workhouses were a constant reminder that in a society without a benefit system the poor, 'deserving' or 'undeserving' as the Victorians deemed them, were only a small step away from effective imprisonment. This situation continued well beyond the reign of Victoria, into the new century, and while many workhouses transitioned into hospitals, the institution itself was not abolished until 1948.

← A view of sleeping female inmates at Lambeth workhouse from a French publication.

DISASTERS & DESTITUTION

↑ The new casual ward at St Marylebone workhouse with its coffin-shaped beds in 1867. These were not typical of all workhouses.

→ An 1890 cartoon from the satirical magazine *Punch* draws attention to the problem of sweated labour.

THE SWEATING SYSTEM EXPOSED
VIRTUAL SLAVERY IN EAST LONDON

In February 1888, Parliament voted to establish a select committee to investigate 'the evils of the sweating system' in London's East End. 'Sweating' was associated with the manufacture of clothing by Jewish immigrants from central and eastern Europe. Sweatshops grew out of the rising demand for ready-to-wear clothes and the decline of the skilled artisan tailor. Manufacturers established small workshops, subcontracted to middlemen, and men and women laboured for long hours in cramped and ill-lit conditions for very low wages.

Parliament noted that the 'condition of the victims of the system might be said, with perfect truth, to be a condition of slavery with all its disadvantages and none of its advantages. The people were practically in a state of servitude, and entirely dependent upon their masters'. The Factory Acts were supposed to protect workers but these were routinely ignored by employers keen to make as much profit as possible.

The sweating system was frequently used by those who opposed immigration to highlight what they saw as imported 'foreign' practice, and a consequence of 'British labour' being driven out of the trade by the influx of cheaper overseas workers. The committee was able to identify the problem but seemingly unable to do much about it. In 1890, it concluded that legislation was 'urgently needed' and this dutifully followed, but since all it did was require employers to keep lists of their out-workers (those who took work home to complete), and local authorities were unable to police the system, little changed until the 1920s.

↑ A hard-hitting satire on sweating from *Punch* that barely disguises its anti-Semitism in its depiction of the sweatshop owner.

ROYAL ARSENAL EXPLOSIONS
THOUSANDS OF BARRELS OF GUNPOWDER SHATTER THE PEACE IN ERITH

On 1 October 1864, three huge explosions shattered the morning peace in the neighbourhoods of Erith, Plumstead and Woolwich, as thousands of barrels of gunpowder ignited. Two gunpowder mills were destroyed, debris was scattered for a mile around, and windows blown out in a four-mile radius of the blasts.

The mills were part of the Royal Arsenal complex at Woolwich, where in excess of 4,000 people worked. Immediately the Arsenal was deluged by wives and children who had rushed over to see if their loved ones were safe. Minutes later, as papers bearing the stamp 'Hall & Sons, Erith' floated to the ground, spread by the blast, it became evident that the explosions had not happened at the Arsenal at all.

As the smoke cleared and rescuers gained access to the devasted mills the extent of the damage and loss of life emerged. Nineteen people were unaccounted for, while another dozen were taken to Guy's Hospital for treatment. Gruesome discoveries were reported by the press, with legs and arms and parts of a shattered human skull recovered hundreds of yards away from the epicentre. The papers speculated that the financial loss of the disaster could run as high as a million pounds (over £100 million today), while 'thousands of pets succumbed with fright, the mortality to canaries being very great'. The Arsenal suffered further damage from explosions in 1883 and 1903, and began to reduce its operations after the First World War, closing its doors in 1967.

← Various scenes showing the explosions at Hall & Sons in Erith.

DISASTERS & DESTITUTION

CORNHILL FIRE OF 1748
LONDON'S UNKNOWN 'GREAT FIRE'

The Great Fire of 1666 is not the only disaster of its type in London's history. In March 1748, a fire that started in a wig shop in Exchange Alley was hugely destructive, bringing down one hundred houses around Cornhill in the City. The fire spread rapidly, chasing across roof rafters and negating the effect of brick party walls, which the 1666 conflagration had caused to be built. It claimed at least six lives, including the family of the wig maker, Mr Eldridge, and a man who broke his back leaping from the flames.

Those caught in the fire rushed to save their possessions, leaving the firefighting to the Fire Insurance Brigades who turned out with 'water engines' to tackle the flames on those properties that had paid their subscriptions. A map of the properties destroyed shows the Eldridge home at the centre of Exchange Alley with a pub (The Three Tuns) and a coffee house nearby. It seems miraculous that so few people died; the nearby 'gunpowder office' on Birching Lane didn't explode, perhaps because it was merely a location from which powder was bought and sold, and not where it was stored.

One individual adversely impacted by the fire was John Ward, who saw the crowds that came to view the ruins on subsequent days as an opportunity for profit. Unfortunately for him he was seen picking a man's pocket and removing a silk handkerchief. Found guilty at the Old Bailey his death sentence was commuted to transportation to the American colonies.

↑ Firefighters tackle the blaze in a contemporary print of the Cornhill Fire.

PIMLICO SEWER DISASTER
DEATH UNDERGROUND

On a Friday evening in October 1849, witnesses reported to Pimlico police that several men were trapped in the Westminster common sewer, running under Warwick Street and Kenilworth Street. PC John Walsh and a surgeon named Wells rushed to see if they could help, descending via a drain cover. Thirty minutes later there was no sign of them, nor of any of the men believed to be underground.

Policemen began digging a hole in the ground to release the noxious air from below. Meanwhile a brave youngster named O'Kay entered the sewer at the opposite end and found constable Walsh. He was pulled out, but was already dead. O'Kay managed to pull another lifeless corpse from the sewers before he himself collapsed from the fumes. Thankfully he recovered, but Dr Wells did not, dying hours later in St George's Hospital.

Work continued long into the night but the rescue crews struggled to cope with the conditions.

In total five people died as a result of exposure to the 'carbonic gas' that filled the tunnels. They had been sent down to measure the level of 'soil' (sewerage), ahead of plans to flush out the sewers. An investigation into the accident analysed the water found in the sewer, and found waste from a nearby gas works which contained sulphuric and prussic acid and ammonia. It was therefore 'not to be wondered at that a very few inhalations [of the fumes] should have caused asphyxia and death'.

↑ Men working underground in the capital's sewer system. This was dangerous work, as the events of October 1849 would show.

THE COLLAPSE OF THE CRYSTAL PALACE
CONSTRUCTION WORKERS FALL FROM THE SKY

In August 1853, workers were busy rebuilding the Crystal Palace which had been moved, piece by piece, from its original home in Hyde Park, where it housed the Great Exhibition of 1851. The Crystal Palace Company had bought the massive glass structure for £70,000 (maybe as much as £7.5 million today), and thousands of workmen were employed installing it at Sydenham, Kent.

On 15 August 1853, horrified witnesses heard a crash and saw the scaffolding surrounding part of the structure collapse, falling 180 feet to the ground. A doctor who rushed to help described seeing men falling from the sky 'like partridges'. The fall killed at least a dozen workers, who were either crushed or who smashed their heads on metalwork. Many more injured were pulled from the wreckage and sent by train to Guy's Hospital.

Some of the bodies were 'shockingly mutilated' as if they had been 'blown up in a mine', the newspapers reported. The collapse of the wood and iron scaffolding also killed a pair of horses and buried the cart they were tethered to.

One of the injured, George Parry (aged 36) sustained two broken legs and a fractured skull. It was reported that in trying to save his life surgeons had attempted trepanning (drilling holes in his skull), but his situation was 'hopeless' and he died, leaving behind wife and six children. Most of the victims had similarly tragic stories. The Crystal Palace never turned a profit for its owners, and it was eventually destroyed by fire in 1936.

↑ The Crystal Palace was one of the wonders of the age and attracted huge crowds.

FIGHTING CHOLERA

DR JOHN SNOW AND THE BROAD STREET PUMP

Several cholera epidemics swept through London in the 1800s. In 1832, cholera killed 5,275 Londoners. In 1848–9, 14,789 died from the infection. 11,661 succumbed in 1853–4, and 5,596 in 1866. Cholera caused stomach cramps, diarrhoea, vomiting and severe dehydration. There was no known cure and it killed millions across the globe. Prevailing medical opinion mistakenly held that cholera was transmitted by miasma ('bad air'), although some scientists argued that cholera was a waterborne disease.

In August 1854, an outbreak of cholera in Soho killed 127 in just three days. Residents fled but the death rate continued to rise, reaching 578. Dr John Snow decided to test the waterborne hypothesis (something he had published on in 1849) by mapping these deaths. He discovered a relationship between fatalities and a water pump in Broad Street. On examining residents at the nearby workhouse, which had its own well, and workers at the Lion Brewery who were given small beer to drink instead of water, he discovered that only five workhouse inmates and none of the brewery workers had succumbed to cholera.

Snow persuaded the authorities to remove the Broad Street pump handle to prevent further deaths. His actions may only have had a limited immediate effect, as the disease had probably run its course, but Snow is credited with a significant breakthrough in demonstrating the connection between polluted water and cholera, even if his hypothesis was rejected at the time. Snow died in 1858, and so did not live to see London's water system overhauled by Sir Joseph Bazalgette (**see page 176**).

↑ A microscope view of microbes and organisms found in London sewer water during the cholera epidemic of 1854.

→→ A powerful image (left) of poor Londoners drinking from the fateful Broad Street pump, with Death operating it. Dr Snow's actions may not have saved their lives but his discovery undoubtedly saved millions in the future. Washing the streets with antiseptic (right).

THE GREAT STINK OF 1858

POLLUTION INTERRUPTS PARLIAMENT

The Thames was Victorian London's key source of fresh water. However, in the 1850s it was in a dreadful state. Sixty sewers emptied their contents directly into its waters, and thick 'black mud' coated the river bed. At low tide at Millbank the banks were covered in a dark sludge. Crisis point was reached in July 1858, during a particularly hot summer.

The river was so polluted that Londoners could no longer ignore the smell emanating from it, and it became a very live issue for politicians in Parliament, who found that the 'stench which arose from the river' made it impossible for them to work there. Discussions of what to do about the problem of sewerage had been ongoing but competing interests, concerns about cost, and a good deal of dithering meant that London suffered decades of inertia on sanitary matters. The cholera outbreaks in 1848 and 1853 (**see page 173**) and the Great Stink of 1858 helped focus minds. In 1855 the Metropolitan Board of Works (MBW) had been created, which had authority across the whole of the capital.

Following the 'Great Stink' the Chancellor of the Exchequer, Benjamin Disraeli, allocated £3 million towards a scheme to overhaul London's sewers, and the MBW tasked their chief engineer, Joseph Bazalgette with the project. By 1863 work had started that would create a new drainage system, and build the new embankments (Victoria to the north and the Albert on the Surrey side) that bordered the River Thames.

THE BETHLEHEM HOSPITAL

BEDLAM, A PLACE OF CONFUSION

As early as the fourteenth century, 'distracted' persons had been locked up in Bethlehem Hospital at Bishopsgate. In 1667 Bethlehem moved to Moorfields, where paupers deemed 'insane' were kept chained up in cages like zoo animals, with little attempt at treatment. From medieval times, local people had shortened 'Bethlehem' to 'Bethlem' which became corrupted to 'Bedlam', and has come to mean 'uproar and confusion' from its association with the hospital.

Bedlam became an attraction for visitors who flocked to see the confined 'lunatics', so much so that in 1770 a ticket system was introduced to control numbers. William Hogarth has left us a powerful image of the chaos of the mid-eighteenth-century institution (see overleaf). The limited understanding of madness in the past meant that patients were bled, purged, whipped, and induced to vomit, on the basis that their 'madness' was occasioned by an imbalance in the four humours (black bile, yellow bile, phlegm and blood). John Howard – the prison reformer – visited Bedlam and saw the awful way inmates were treated. He gave his voice to existing concerns over the conditions in Bedlam, which echoed those across the wider prison estate.

In 1815 a new hospital was constructed in Lambeth, and Bedlam's 122 inmates were transferred there. Criminal lunatics were admitted from 1835 until 1864, when Broadmoor Prison opened in Berkshire. Bedlam continued to treat the mentally ill until 1930, when its patients were moved to Beckenham. The Lambeth site has been occupied by the Imperial War Museum since 1936.

↑ An inmate in Bedlam; very little 'care' was offered to those confined there.

→ William Hogarth's disturbing image of patients inside Bedlam, from 'A Rake's Progress'.

DISASTERS & DESTITUTION

THE SILVERTOWN MUNITIONS EXPLOSION

LONDON'S LARGEST EXPLOSION

By 1915, Britain was embroiled in a 'war to end all wars' and Lloyd George, as head of the Ministry of Munitions, was responsible for ensuring troops had enough armaments to fight Germany and her allies. Silvertown, on the River Thames between Bow Creek and Barking Creek, was a hub of industry in the late Victorian period. Brunner Mond's chemical factory at Crescent Wharf had manufactured caustic soda until it closed in 1912 but remained ripe for redeployment.

Lloyd George determined that every avenue for explosives manufacture had to be explored, even those that constituted a risk to life and property given the danger associated with the process. Therefore, in September 1915 Brunner Mond's 268 employees began producing TNT for the war effort. On the 19 January 1917, disaster struck when fire ignited fifty tons of explosives, blowing up the factory and damaging 70,000 properties in its vicinity. Seventy-three people were killed and hundreds of others injured by the blast, but observers were amazed that the death toll was as low as it was.

There were dark rumours that enemy agents had set the fire, but a government inquiry concluded that the cause was probably more mundane, either a spark from one element of the process had ignited the explosive or it had combusted spontaneously. The cost of the damages ran into the hundreds of thousands of pounds and the Silvertown explosion remains the largest single incident of its kind to happen in the capital's history.

↑ A contemporary photograph of the devastating effects of the Silvertown explosion, where 73 people lost their lives.

DEBTORS' PRISONS
FAMILIES IMPRISONED FOR RUNNING OUT OF CREDIT

London had a number of prisons housing those unable to pay their debts. Debtors' gaols had originally accommodated those who owed a debt to the monarch, but by the eighteenth century it was the 'middling sorts' (middle class) who were imprisoned. Creditors actively pursued debtors, using a process that had existed since medieval times, allowing them to have debtors imprisoned until accounts were settled. Debtors were tracked down by informers and 'bum-bailiffs' who carried them off to 'spunging houses' to be persuaded to pay up or face prison.

However, prisons like the Fleet and Marshalsea, the Queen's Bench and Whitecross Street gaol in the City, were probably providing a crude form of sanctuary for some people who couldn't afford to service the debts they had run up. Being locked up for debt might seem a terrible injustice, but not everyone suffered. Well-to-do prisoners, those with friends and family on the outside who could supply food, drink and, crucially, money, might carry on as they had before they were incarcerated.

And plenty lived with their families in gaol, as Charles Dickens' father had when he was sent to the Marshalsea Prison in 1824. In 1819 the Fleet prison on Farringdon Street held 250 debtors, plus thirty-five wives and fifty-four children. 1842 saw the closure of the Marshalsea and the Fleet. Queen's Bench and Whitecross Street followed in 1869 when the Debtors' Act reduced the courts' powers to lock up debtors, but it was not until the 1900s that the practice ceased entirely.

↑ An illustration of Fleet Prison by Robert Cruikshank.

THE GIN CRAZE

DRUNK FOR A PENNY; DEAD DRUNK FOR TWO-PENCE

In 1751 William Hogarth published a pair of artworks, *Gin Lane* (see opposite) and *Beer Street*. Hogarth intended them as his visual contribution to a long-running campaign against the consumption of cheap gin (or 'geneva' as it was also called). In the first half of the eighteenth century, many Londoners were drinking huge amounts of this cheaply produced spirit. Commentators were appalled at the destructive nature of the so-called 'gin craze' on society, as Hogarth's drawing so dramatically illustrated.

Parliament had attempted to curb sales of gin in 1736 by requiring vendors to obtain a licence at the prohibitive cost of £50, fining those unable or unwilling to do so. This resulted in rioting as the crowd turned on informers, who had hoped to profit from the £5 reward offered for the successful prosecution of unlicensed sellers. The 1736 Gin Act was pretty ineffectual, and consumption continued apace, prompting several more acts of parliament, none of which stemmed the flow of gin.

In the end Hogarth's prints probably had more effect, contrasting as they did the perils of geneva to the benefits of beer which was, patriotically of course, more *English*. Moreover, gin declined as a cheap option for drinkers from about 1757 due to the rising price of grain.

Gin drinking was revived in the later 1800s with the proliferation of 'Gin Palaces'. Once again, the capital's drinkers could be 'drunk for a penny' and 'dead drunk for two-pence'.

←← A satirical print from 1829 makes the destructive danger of gin transparently clear as the figure of Death enters a gin shop.

↑ Perhaps William Hogarth's most famous engraving, *Gin Lane*, which did so much to draw attention to the problem of alcohol abuse in Georgian London.

DISASTERS & DESTITUTION 183

COLNEY HATCH HOSPITAL

AN ASYLUM FOR THE MODERN AGE

While the treatment of the mentally ill could hardly be said to be either effective or considerate in the Victorian period, there was a marked improvement on previous centuries of abuse and the use of madness as 'entertainment' (**see page 176**). In July 1851, a new institution opened at Friern Barnet: the Middlesex County Lunatic Asylum, known more often as Colney Hatch.

Originally built to house 1,000 patients, it was expanded to reach a capacity of 2,500 by the end of the 1800s, making it the largest asylum in Europe. Despite being purpose built, Colney Hatch was still a very unpleasant place for many of its inmates, especially by the 1880s when conditions were reportedly very poor. The number of chronically ill and eldery patients necessitated the building of a temporary set of new dormitories in 1896, but this wood and corrugated iron structure was burned to the ground in 1903, claiming the lives of fifty-two female inmates.

The asylum has been associated with a number of famous inmates, including three men suspected of being Jack the Ripper. The most enduring of these (in terms of his prominence as a Ripper suspect at least) was Aaron Kosminski (or simply 'Kosminsky' as he is inscribed in Melville Macnaghten's much-quoted memorandum). Kosminski was admitted to Colney Hatch on 7 February 1891, aged 23, and his condition was recorded as 'mania'.

The hospital closed in 1993, after decades of decline, and was converted into luxury accommodation and a private gymnasium.

THE FOREST GATE SCHOOL FIRE

A TRAGIC START TO THE NEW YEAR

In the 1840s and 1850s concerns about juvenile crime and delinquency were addressed in proposals put forward by Mary Carpenter and the Reformatory Movement. Carpenter believed that working-class boys and girls were being failed by society, and their descent into criminality was not an inherent moral failing on their part, but something which intervention could prevent and ameliorate. As a result, Parliament legislated to create Reformatory and Industrial Schools. Children found begging could be sent to an industrial school, as could orphans, truants and youngsters found in brothels or those whose parents were seen as unfit to look after them.

One Industrial School was built at Forest Gate on the instructions of the Whitechapel Board of Guardians (of the Poor). Tragedy struck on New Year's Day 1890 when, while eighty-four boys slept, fire raged through two dormitories in a detached part of the site. The matron had checked all lights were out and everything 'seemed safe', but at twenty past midnight she smelled burning. She raced to the dormitory and raised the alarm but by then the fire had taken and smoke filled the rooms.

Despite the best efforts of the staff and firemen, as well as nearby railway workers, not all the boys were saved. Twenty-six children, aged seven to twelve, died from suffocation. Thereafter new rules for fire prevention and detection were rolled out across the similar institutions in London, including fire drills and (later) direct telephone links to the fire brigade.

→ *The Graphic* newspaper portrays distressed relatives gathering at the inquest on its front page (bottom).

THE GRAPHIC

AN ILLUSTRATED WEEKLY NEWSPAPER

No. 1,050—Vol. XLI
Registered as a Newspaper

SATURDAY, JANUARY 11, 1890

WITH EXTRA SUPPLEMENT

PRICE SIXPENCE
By Post 6½d.

THE BURNING OF LAEKEN CASTLE, BRUSSELS, THE RESIDENCE OF KING LEOPOLD

THE DISASTROUS FIRE AT FOREST GATE DISTRICT SCHOOL—THE RELATIVES OF THE VICTIMS AT THE INQUEST

ABOUT THE AUTHOR

Drew Gray was born in Islington in the 1960s. As a child growing up in North London, he developed a love of reading and history, and a fascination with his home city. Drew was awarded a PhD in 2006 from the University of Northampton for his thesis exploring the City of London's magistracy in the late 1700s. Since then, he has taught the history of crime at the university, given many public lectures, and appeared on numerous TV and radio programmes and podcasts. He has published eight books, including: *Murder Maps: Crime Scenes Revisited* (Thames & Hudson, 2020), *London's Shadows: The Dark Side of the Victorian City* (Bloomsbury, 2010), and *Nether World: Crime and the Police Courts in Victorian London* (Reaktion, 2024). Drew still lives in North London and is a long-suffering Arsenal fan, a keen amateur photographer and an occasional gardener.

ACKNOWLEDGEMENTS

Historians spend a considerable amount of time in archives and libraries and my research for *Dark London* was no exception. Yet we can easily forget that everything has to be catalogued, located and delivered to the reading rooms, then safely collected, checked off and returned. Those who work in The London Archives and at The British Library do this quietly and efficiently, without fuss, and with considerable care both for the items and the researchers. They are knowledgeable, polite and, above all, patient. So they deserve all of our thanks, and especially those at The British Library who have had to cope with the increased pressure caused by a cyber-attack.

I would also like to thank the team at Quarto, especially Katerina Menhennet for supporting me through all the various stages, and to John Parton for trusting me with his idea for *Dark London*. I hope the finished product is everything they wished for.

Researching new areas always throws up challenges and so I would like to thank my colleague and friend Dr Caroline Nielsen for her advice on the supernatural world, and in particular for opening my eyes to the Cock Lane ghost story. As ever all mistakes are entirely my own.

Lastly, I would like to thank London and all who have made it what it is, the greatest city in the world. It is always evolving and has been built by migration and the ideas, skills and determination of those who choose it as their home. As Edward Rutherford wrote, a Londoner is 'someone who lives here'.

FURTHER READING

If you have been inspired to find out more about the stories in *Dark London* or the history of the capital, then you could do worse than start with Peter Ackroyd's sweeping narrative *London: The Biography* (2000).

For the eighteenth and nineteenth centuries, I have found Jerry White's twin studies (2007 and 2012) excellent reading, while M. Dorothy George's *London Life in the Eighteenth Century* (1925), although old, remains a fascinating study. More recent is *London Lives: Poverty, Crime and the Making of a Modern City, 1690–1800* by Tim Hitchcock and Robert Shoemaker, who trace the city's history through the records of the criminal justice system. The book links to their companion website www.londonlives.org and to one of the best and free online resources for the study of crime and policing in London, www.oldbaileyonline.org, where you will be able access criminal trials from the 1680s to the early 1900s.

If the chapter on crime and punishment has piqued your interest, then may I humbly recommend my own *Nether World: Crime and the Police Courts in Victorian London* (2024) for a deep dive into crime and criminality through the pages of nineteenth-century newspapers.

I found Steve Roud's *London Lore: The Legends and Traditions of the World's Most Vibrant City* (2008) a great primer for the oddities of London's history. For the supernatural world see Owen Davies' *The Haunted: A Social History of Ghosts* (2007), Roger Clarke's *A Natural History of Ghosts: 500 Years of Hunting for Proof* (2012), and Paul Chambers', *The Cock Lane Ghost: Murder, Sex & Haunting in Dr Johnson's London* (2006) for what is one of the most curious stories associated with London.

Lastly, if you like to delve into much older volumes to explore the history some of these stories engage with, then seek out Henry Mayhew's *The Criminal Prisons of London and Scenes of Prison Life* (1862), or the six volumes of G. W. Thornbury's *Old and New London* (c. 1873).

INDEX

Page numbers in *italics* refer to illustrations.

A

Abberline, Detective Inspector Frederick 36
Abney Park burial ground 82
Acton, William 131
Albert, Prince of Saxe-Coburg and Gotha 60, 62
alcoholism 144, 148, 182, *182*, 183
Allen, PC Joseph 136
Almack's club 122, 132
Alsop, Jane 100
Anderson, Amy, *see* Fay, Tottie
animal cruelty 125, *125*-7
Anne, Queen 66, 120
Archer, Richard 52
Armstrong, Eliza 114
Ashbee, Henry Spencer 141, *141*
    My Secret Life 141

B

Bacon, George W.
    New Large Scale Ordnance Atlas of London & Suburbs 165
Ball, Thomas 157
Balsamo, Giuseppe, *see* Cagliostro
the Bank of England 22, 65, 77
Barrett, Michael 34, 67
Bartholomew Fair 118, *118*
Baum, Frederick 71
Bazalgette, Sir John 173, 176
Bean, John William 60
Bedlam asylum 60, 176, *177*-9
beer flood, *see* Horseshoe Brewery
Bell, Reverend William 18
Bellingham, John 49, *49*
Bentham, Jeremy 51
50, Berkeley Square 94
Berkeley, Elizabeth 136
Berry: James 72
    John 66
Bethlehem Hospital, *see* Bedlam asylum

Bethnal Green gang, graverobbers 110
Bidwell, Austin and George 22, *22*, 23
Bishop, John 110
Blake, William 76
Blavatsky, Madame Helena Petrovna 83, 86, 87
blood sports 125, *126*, 127
Boleyn, Anne 94, 95
Boodle's club 122
Boswell, James
    Life of Samuel Johnson 104
Boulton, Ernest 133, *133*-5
Bow Street
    police court 14, 44, 57, 83, 133
    runners 14, 24, 42
Bravo, Florence and Charles 64, *64*
Brixton
    baby farmers 63, *63*
    prison 50
Broadmoor prison 52, 62, 148, 177
Brompton burial ground 82
Brooks, Sergeant 27
Brooks's club 122
Brown, Hannah 33
Brunel, Marc and Isambard 157
Bullock, William 92
Bunhill Fields 76, *76*
Bunyan, John 76
burial grounds 76, 82, *82*, 86, 102, 103
Burke, William 110
burkers, *see* graverobbing 110
Burns, Bill 125, *125*
Burr, William 146
Burton, Harry 36
Buxton, Thomas Fowell 76
SS *Bywell Castle* 149

C

Cadwell & Co., firework factory 160
Cagliostro, Count Alessandro di 81, *81*
the Camberwell ghost 107, *107*
Cambridge, Duke of 102
Camden, George 82
Camden Town, murder 29, *29*
Campbell, Robert 48
Cardigan, Lord 59
Carpenter, Mary 184
Cashin, Ellen and Catherine 128
Chapman, 'Dark' Annie 30
Charing Cross, pillory 16, *17*, 138

Chauvet, Lewis 48
the Chelsea ghost 80, *80*
cholera 173, *173*-5, 176
Churchill, Winston 39, *40*, *41*
Clarke, Daniel 48
Clerkenwell Prison, bombing 34, *34*, 35, 67
the Cleveland Street scandal 116
Cockburn, Lord Chief Justice 36
the Cock Lane ghost 88, *88*, 89, *89*
Coldbath Fields Prison, Clerkenwell 27, *27*, 42, 70, 145
Coles, Frances 30
Collins, John 157
Colney Hatch Hospital 184
Colquhon, Patrick 42
Cooke
    George Alfred 92
    Jeptha 157
Cooper, Eleanor
Cornhill, fire, 1748 170, *170*
Cornwell, Patricia 29
correction, houses of 70, *70*, 71, 138, 163
    see also, prisons
courtroom, Victorian 9
courts, police 14, *14*, 15
    see also, Bow Street
Covent Garden 52, 104, 128
Cowen, John Walter 63
Cowland, Edward 164
Cox, Jane 64
Crippen
    Cora 56
    Hawley Harvey 56, 57, *57*
Crockford, William 122
cross dressing 133, *133*-5, 138, 140
Cruikshank, Robert
    Fleet prison 181
Crystal Palace disaster 172, *172*
Culley, PC Robert 27, *27*
Cunningham, James Gilbert 36
Cuper's pleasure gardens 120

D

Dakin, William 80, *80*
Dance, George, the Younger 67
Davis, Alfred 146
debtors' prisons 181, *181*

188 DARK LONDON

Defoe, Daniel 17, 18
  Robinson Crusoe 76
d'Éon, Charles (Charlotte) 140, *140*
de Roux, Maria 43
Derrick, Samuel 128
de Sade, Marquis
  Justine 112
detective department, *see* police
Dew, Chief Inspector Walter 56, 57
Dickens, Charles 144, 181
  Bleak House 43
  The Haunted Man and the Ghost's Bargain 90
  Oliver Twist 147
Dimmock, Emily 'Phyllis' 29
Dircks, Henry 90
disease, *see* cholera, plague, typhus
Disraeli, Benjamin 176
Dodd, Thomas 15
Donkin, Dr Bryan 83
drug use 62, 110
drunkenness, *see* alcoholism
Drury Lane, Theatre Royal 106
duelling 58, 59
the Dynamitards 34
Dyson, Arthur 45

E

Eastman, William 48
Eddowes, Catherine 'Kate' 30
the Egyptian Hall 92, *92*
Egyptology 92, 103
Eldridge, wig maker 170
the elephant man, *see* Merrick
Ellis
  John 57
  Sarah 63
Ellmore, Belle, *see* Crippen, Cora
Erith, explosion 169, *169*
Evans, Thomas 157
executioners 44, 45, 57, 72
'Fanny and Stella', *see* Boulton, Park
Faraday, Michael 90
Fawcett, Lieutenant-Colonel David 59
Fawkes, Guy 94
Fay, Tottie 148, *148*
Feliciani, Lorenza Seraphina 81
Fenians, *see* Irish republicanism
Ferrers, Laurence Shirley, 4th Earl 19, *19–21*

Field, George 138
Fielding, Henry and John 14, 24
firework factory explosion 160, *160*
Floyd, Charles 164
Ford, Parson 104, *104*, 105
Forest Gate, school fire 184, 185
fortune telling 96–9, *97*
Francis, John 60
Freemasonry 81, 87
Fry, Elizabeth 67

G

Gale, Sarah 33, *33*
gambling 118, 120, 122, *122*, *123*, 125, *125*
gaol fever, *see* typhus
Gardstein, George 39
George, Lloyd 180
George III 65
Gillray, James 81
gin, *see* alcoholism
Girdler, William 78
Goldsmith, Oliver
  She Stoops to Conquer 89
Good, Daniel 44, *44*
Gordon, Lord George 65
  the Gordon Riots, 1780 24, 65, *65*, 67
Gowan, James 42
Graham, 'Dr' James 124
graverobbing 110, *111*
Graves, John Henry 52
the 'Great Stink', 1858 176
Greenacre, James 33, *33*
Greenwood, James 165
Grey, Lady Jane 94, 95
Griffin, James 154
Griffiths, suicide 86
Grimaldi, Joseph 106, *106*
Gubert, Millie and Isaac 161
Gully, Dr 64

H

Hall & Sons, Erith, explosion 169, *169*
Hamilton, William 60, 62
the Hammersmith ghost 78, *78*, 79
Hampstead 110
  tragedy 72, *73*
Hare, William 110
Harrington, Bridget 42
Harriott, John 42

Harris
  Harry 39
  Jack (*List of Covent Garden Ladies*) 128
Hebrew Dramatic Club, disaster 161
Hefeld, Paul 38
Highgate Cemetery 82, *84*, *85*
highwaymen 18, 19, 24, 66
Hill, Susannah 112, *112*
Hogarth, William 89
  Beer Street 182, *183*
  'The Four Stages of Cruelty', 1750–111, 125, *127*
  Gin Lane 144, 182, *183*
  'A Harlot's Progress' *131*
  A Midnight Modern Conversation, 1732 104, 105
  'A Rake's Progress' *177*, *178*, *179*
Hogg, Phoebe, Frank and Tiggy 72
Holloway 56
  prison 51, 52, 70, 71, 72, 114
Holywell Street 113, *113*
Hooke, Dr Robert 162
Horseshoe Brewery accident 152
Horwood, Lucy 160
Houndsditch 39
Howard, John 51, 177
hulks, *see* prison hulks
the Hummums 104, *104*, 105
Hyde Park pet cemetery 102, *102*
Hyndman, Henry 157

I

insanity, *see* Bedlam asylum, Broadmoor prison, Colney Hatch Hospital
Irish Republicanism 34, 36, 60, 62
Irving, Henry 52

J

'Jack the Ripper', *see* Whitechapel murders
James I 94
Jarrett, Rebecca 114
Jenkins, Thomas 162
Johnson
  Dr Samuel 104
  John 19
Jones, Jane 44
Joscelyne, Ralph 38

K

Kelly, Mary Jane 29, 30
Kendall, Captain of the *Montrose* 56
Kensal Green burial ground 82
Kent, William 88, 89
Keyworth, Albert 38
Knox, Robert 110
Kosminski, Aaron 184
Kotzwara (Kočvara), Francis 112, *112*
Krotofsky family 161

L

Lambeth workhouse 165, *165*
Lane, Harriett 36
Lankester, Professor Ray 83
laudanum, *see* drug use
Leeson, Detective Sergeant Ben 39
Le Neve, Ethel 56, 57, *57*
Leno, Dan 106
Lepidus, Jacob 38
Linnell, Alfred 157
Lombard Street, bullion robbery 71, *71*
London Bridge, 1852 7
London Museum 92
Long
    'Dr' John St John 128, *129*
    John 157
lottery, state, the Guildhall 123
Louis XVI 140
Lynes, Fanny 88

M

macaronis 132, *132*
MacDonnell, George 22
Macklin, Charles 106
Maclean, Roderick *61*, 62
Macnaughten, Melville 184
Major, John, fortune teller 97
Manning, Maria and Frederick 43, *43*
Mansfield, Lord 89
Marble Arch, *see* Tyburn gallows
Marie Antoinette 81
Marr, Timothy and Celia 42
Marrow, Ann 138
Marylebone
    pleasure gardens 120
    workhouse 166
Maskelyne, John Nevil 83, 92
May, James, graverobber 110
Mayhew, Henry 70, 71

Mayne, Richard 26
McDaniel, Stephen, and gang 24, 66
Melbourne, Lord 27, 60
mental illness, *see* Bedlam asylum, Broadmoor prison, Colney Hatch Hospital
Merrick, Joseph Carey, the elephant man 119, *119*
Methveston, *see* Major
Metropolitan police, *see* police
Metyard, Sarah 147
Millbank prison 50, 70
Millward, Jessie 52
Milward, Thomas 78, *79*
Mond, Brunner 180
Monroe, Lieutenant Alexander 59
the 'Monster' 28, *28*
the Monument 162, *162*
Moore, Rev. 88, 89
Morgan
    Ellen 97
    Sarah 147
Mortality, Bills of 153
Moyes, Margaret, suicide 162

N

Nailor, Ann and Mary 147
Nero, Tom 11
Newgate prison and executions 15, 28, 33, 34, 44, 49, 65, 67, *67–9*, 77, 110, 145
Newlove, Henry 116
'New Police', *see* police, Metropolitan
Nichols, Mary Ann 'Polly' 30
Norwood burial ground 82
Noyes, Edwin 22
Nunhead burial ground 82

O

O'Connor
    Arthur 62
    Patrick 43
O'Kay, sewer disaster 171
Olcott, Colonel Harry Steel 87
the Old Bailey 15, 22, 27–9, 36, 49, 67, 77, 78, 88, 97, 110, 112, 128, 145, 170
Oliver, Elizabeth Howell 76
Oxford, Edward 60

P

Page, Dame Mary 76
Pall Mall 81, 124, 157, *158*, *159*
Park, Frederick 133, *133–5*
Parliament, the Houses of 36, 65
Parry, George 172
Parsons, Richard and Elizabeth 88, 89
Pate, Robert 62
Peace, Charles 45, *45*
Pearcey, Mary 72, *73*
Peckham, ghosts 107
Peel, Robert 24, 26, 44
Pentonville prison 45, 50, 67, 70, 145
Pepper, John Henry, ghost 90, *90*
Perceval, Spencer, shooting of 49, *49*
pet cemetery 102, *102*
Peter, the Painter 39
phantasmagoria 93, *93*
Philidor, Paul 93
Phillips, George Bagster 161
the pillory *16*, 17, *17*, 18, 66, 89, 138
Pimlico, sewer disaster 171, *171*
Pinkerton, George 22
plague 76, 152
pleasure gardens 120, *120*
police 24–7, *24–27*, 65, 78, 110, *111*, 144
    courts 14, 117
    Metropolitan 26, 27, 30, 33, *38–41*, 44, 122, 138, 157, 163, 171
    detective department 44, 46, 47, 56, 71
    Thames River 42
    see also, Bow Street
Poor Laws, *see* workhouses
Pope, Alexander, ghost 91, *91*
    Sandy's Ghost 91
pornography 112, 113, 141
Porter, Anne and Sarah 28
Primrose Hill necropolis 103, *103*
Prince, Richard, *see* Archer, Richard
SS *Princess Alice*, disaster 149, *149–51*, 154
prisons 50, *50*, 51, *51*, 67–70, 145
    prison hulks 53, *53–5*
    see also, Bedlam; Brixton; Broadmoor; Clerkenwell; Coldbath; Colney Hatch Hospital; correction, houses of; debtors' prisons; Holloway; Millbank, Newgate; Pentonville;

Tothill Fields; Wandsworth; workhouses
prostitution 17, 29, 104, 112, 114, 116, *116*, *117*, 118, 120, 128, *130*, 131, 136, *136*, 138, *138*, 141, 148

R
railway crash, see Wood Green
Raleigh, Sir Walter 94
Ranelagh pleasure gardens 120, *121*
Rann, John 'Sixteen String Jack' 18, *18*
the Ratcliffe Highway murders 42, 86
Regent's Park skating disaster, 1867 154, *154*, 155
Ricardo, Alexander 64
Robertson, Etienne-Gaspard 93
Robin, Henri 92
Rowan, Charles 26
Rowlandson, Thomas
   Cock fight, 1808 *126*
Royal Arsenal explosions 169, *169*

S
Sawyer, Rose 160
Scales, Lucy 100
Seton, William 157
sexual health, advice 124
Shaw, Bertram 29
Sickert, Walter 29
Sidney Street, the Siege of 39, *39*
Silvertown munitions explosion 180
Sims, Eliza 80
Skudder, Susanna 136
Slade, Henry and Emily 83, *83*
Smith: Francis 78, *79*
   manager, Hebrew Dramatic Club 161
Smithfield Market 17, 88, 115, 118, 125
Smyth, Mrs Maria 28
Snow, Dr John 173
Sokoloff, William 39
Solomons, Isaac (Ikey), Henry and Ann 15, *15*
spiritualism 83, 87
Spitalfields 30, 110, 161
   weavers 48, *48*
Spring-heeled Jack 100, *101*, 107
Spurzheim, Johann 91
Stead, William T. 114, *114*
Stewart, William 72

St Giles Rookery 144, *144*, 152
St James 36
Stokes, Alfred 36
Strachan, Charles
Strangling, an Essay on the Art of (pamphlet) 112
Stride, Elizabeth 'Long Liz' 30
Stroud, Henry 48
Stuart, Lady Arbella 94
suicide 38, 86, 162, 164
Svaars, Fritz 39
sweatshops 168, *168*

T
Tabram, Martha 30
Taylor, William 36
Tenniel, John 90
Terriss, William, murder 52, *52*
Thackeray, William Makepeace 43
Thames Tunnel flooding 156, 157
Theatre Royal, see Drury Lane
Thornton, Eliza and Elizabeth 160
Tothill Fields prison 70, *70*
the Tottenham Court Road gas explosion 146, *146*, *147*
the Tottenham Outrage, 1910 38, *38*, 39
Tower Hamlets burial ground 82
the Tower of London 19, 36, 94, 95
Trafalgar Square 36
   riots 157, *158*, *159*
transgender 140
Treves, Dr Frederick 119
Turner, John 42
Turpin, Dick 18
Tyburn gallows 18, 19, 67, 147
Tyler, PC William 38
typhus 145

V
Vagrancy Acts, 1822 and 1824 138, 163
Vauxhall pleasure gardens 120, *120*
Veck, George 116
Victoria, Queen 52, 102, 119
   assassination attempts 60, *61*, 624

W
Wainwright, Henry and Thomas 36, 37

Walsh, PC John 171
Walthamstow 110
Wandsworth prison 51, 70, 71
Wapping 42
Ward, John 170
Warren, Charles 157
watchmen, see police
Waterford, Marquis of 100
Waters, Margaret 63, *63*
Wellington, Duke of 59, 157
Wells, Dr, sewer disaster 171
Whitechapel murders 29, 30, *30*–32, 36, *37*, 57, 72, 100, 131, 161, 184
Whitehead, Paul and Sarah 77, *77*
White's club 122
wife selling 115, *115*
Wilberforce, William 163
Wild, Jonathan 24, 66
Williams
   John 42, 86
   Rhynwick 28
   Thomas 110
Williamson, John and Elizabeth 42
Wilson
   James 38
   Thomas 103
Winbridge, Hyde Park gatekeeper 102
Wood
   Robert 29, *29*
   Susanna, see Skudder
Wood Green, railway crash 164, *164*
Woolwich 149, 169
workhouses 50, 71, 110, 119, 147, 165, 165–7, 173
Wren, Sir Christopher 67, 162

INDEX 191

PICTURE CREDITS

Mary Evans Picture Library 4, 16–17, 19, 27, 30, 31 (left), 43, 45, 49, 50–51, 52, 54–55, 58–59, 65, 66, 68–69, 70, 76, 78, 79, 81, 87, 90, 91, 92, 93, 99, 101, 106, 113, 120, 122–123, 125, 126, 130, 134–135, 136, 139, 140, 144, 150–151, 156, 162, 165, 168, 172, 174, 177, 181, 182; PATSTOCK/Getty 7; duncan1890/Getty 8; wynnter/Getty 11; © Illustrated London News Ltd/Mary Evans 14, 22, 23, 29, 32, 34–35, 53, 56, 56–57, 60–61, 64, 67, 83, 98, 102, 137, 149, 154–155, 158–159, 161, 163, 166, 171; State Library of New South Wales 15; Reading Room 2020/Alamy Stock Photo 18; Mary Evans/Peter & Dawn Cope Collection 20–21, 82, 121; Mary Evans Picture Library/GROSVENOR PRINTS 24; ©Metropolitan Police Authority/Mary Evans 25, 26, 39, 46–47, 111; ©Florilegius/Mary Evans 28, 77; © John Frost Newspapers/Mary Evans Picture Library 31 (top); © Mary Evans/Sueddeutsche Zeitung Photo~~ 31 (right); Chronicle/Alamy Stock Photo 33; From the British Library archive/Bridgeman Images 37, 63, 72–73, 80; 107, 112, 116–117, 146–147, 148, 160, 164, 169; Mary Evans/Pharcide 38, 40–41; Heritage Image Partnership Ltd/Alamy Stock Photo 44, 115, 170, 180; The History Emporium/Alamy Stock Photo 48; Look and Learn/Peter Jackson Collection/Bridgeman Images 71, 124; De Luan/Alamy Stock Photo 84–85; Mary Evans/Library of Congress 88–89; The Print Collector/Alamy Stock Photo 95, 153, 185; Authentic-Originals/Alamy Stock Photo 96–97; Antiqua Print Gallery/Alamy Stock Photo 103; The Metropolitan Museum of Art, Gift of Sarah Lazarus, 1891 104–105; Alpha Stock/Alamy Stock Photo 114; Hein Nouwens/Getty 118; ©Photo Researchers/Mary Evans Picture Library 119; The Metropolitan Museum of Art, Harris Brisbane Dick Fund, 1932, 127, 183; Coloured etching attributed to A. Sharpshooter, 1830. Source: Wellcome Collection 129; © The Trustees of the British Museum 132; History and Art Collection/Alamy Stock Photo 133; Volgi archive/Alamy Stock Photo 141; Mary Evans/Peter Higginbotham Collection 145; The Picture Art Collection/Alamy Stock Photo 147 (bottom); World History Archive/Mary Evans Picture Library 167; Wellcome Images/Science Source/Mary Evans 173; duncan1890/Getty 175; William Hogarth, British, 1697–1764/Published by William Hogarth, British, 1697–1764/Scene in Bedlam, 1735, printed 1763/Etching and engraving/plate: 35.7 x 40.7 cm. (14 1/16 x 16 in.)/sheet: 49 x 65.5 cm (19 5/16 x 25 13/16 in.)/Princeton University Art Museum. Gift of Mrs. William H. Walker II/x1988-37 178–179.